AF267418

# THE ENTREPRENEURIAL MINDSET

## 13 SECRETS TO YOUR SUCCESS

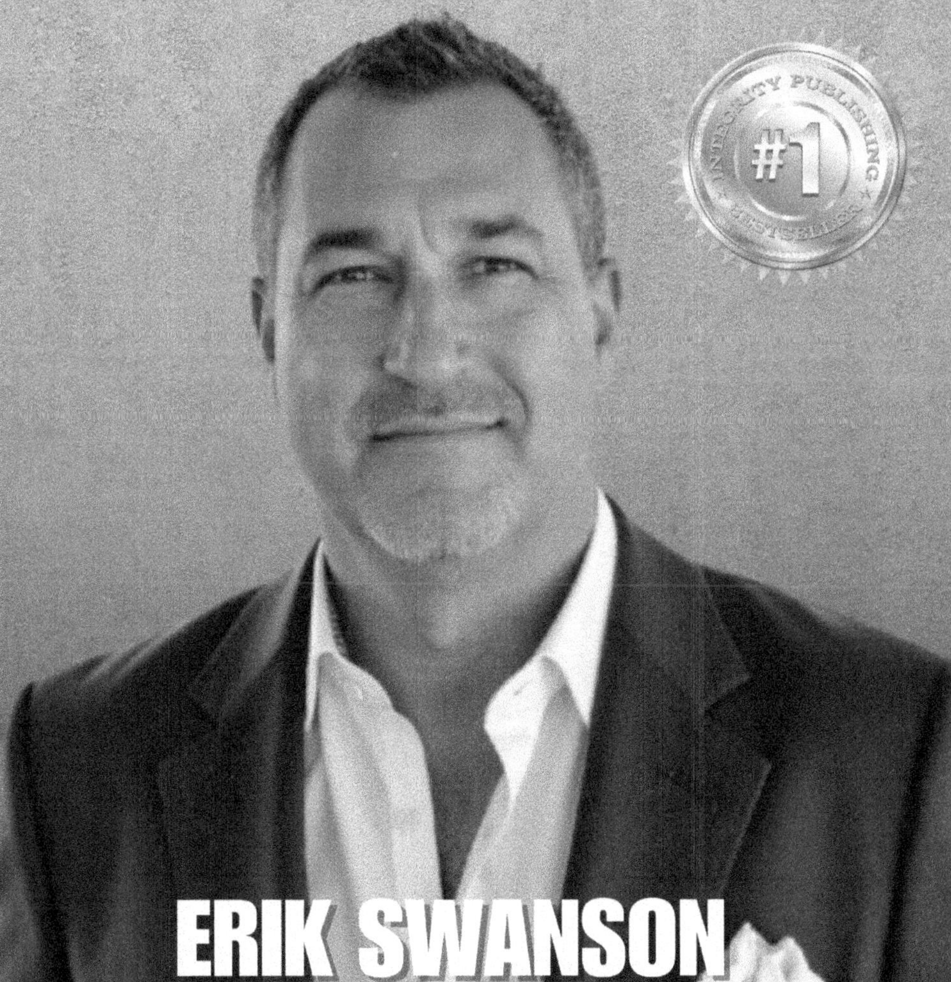

# ERIK SWANSON

## INTERNATIONAL #1 BESTSELLING AUTHOR

**Integrity Publishing International LLC**

**Copyright © 2026**

**THE ENTREPRENEUR MINDSET | ERIK SWANSON**

**Published by Integrity Publishing International LLC**
*www.IntegrityPub.com*



Orders by U.S. trade bookstores and wholesalers.

Email: *Team@IntegrityPub.com*

Paperback ISBN: 978-1-964330-56-3
Hardcover ISBN: 978-1-964330-57-0

# *TESTIMONIALS FOR BESTSELLER ERIK SWANSON*

"Entrepreneurship is not just about strategy—it's about mindset and frequency and how you show up for the world. Erik Swanson's newest book, ***The Entrepreneurial Mindset***, delivers powerful messages and secrets on how successful entrepreneurs think, act, and grow."

—***Dr. Joe Vitale*** ~ NY Times Bestselling Author, Featured in book and movie The Secret

"Erik Swanson combines motivation with real entrepreneurial wisdom. ***The Entrepreneurial Mindset*** is a powerful guide for anyone who wants to stop surviving and start thriving in business and life."

—***Larry Namer*** ~ Founder of E! Entertainment Television, Bestselling Author

"Erik Swanson has a gift for turning powerful ideas into practical action. This book will inspire you to think differently, execute boldly, and lead with purpose."

—***Jeff Hoffman*** ~ Entrepreneur, Speaker, Humanitarian, Bestselling Author, Startup of Priceline

"What makes Erik Swanson special is not just his knowledge—it's the genuine care he has for people. In ***The Entrepreneurial Mindset***, he encourages readers to believe in themselves, grow through challenges, and pursue their vision with courage and confidence."

—**Rita Davenport** ~ Co-Founder (NSA) National Speakers Association, Former President Arbonne International

"Looking for a great book to propel your life in the right way for success? Grab Erik Swanson's newest book *The Entrepreneurial Mindset* and watch your life grow in amazing ways!"

—*Greg S. Reid* ~ Bestselling Author, Speaker, Founder of Secret Knock

"My great friend Awesome Erik is prolific and has integrity and wonderment of his daily life in this world. He sees things differently than other people, and is someone who really lives the meaning of 'to take a moment and smell the roses.' His insight is necessary for people to hear. It will uplift and change lives."

—*Claudia Wells* ~ Actor, Entrepreneur, Owner of Armani Wells

"This book will challenge the way you think about success. Erik Swanson delivers powerful lessons, real-world insights, and practical strategies that every entrepreneur needs in today's fast-moving world."

—*Dr. Steve Taubman* ~ Magician, Bestselling Author, Hypnotist

"Erik Swanson delivers a powerful reminder that the greatest asset any entrepreneur possesses is their mindset. This book will inspire you to think bigger, take action faster, and pursue your goals with relentless determination."

—*Jen Du Plessis* ~ Bestselling Author, Speaker

"Erik Swanson speaks directly to the heart of entrepreneurship. In his book, *The Entrepreneurial Mindset,* Erik shares a powerful reminder that success begins in the mind before it ever shows up in your bank account."

—*Patrick Carney* ~ "The Artiste"

"Erik Swanson has done it again. *The Entrepreneurial Mindset* is more than a book—it's a blueprint for thinking, acting, and winning like a true entrepreneur. If you're ready to elevate your mindset and your business, this book is a must-read."

—*Bill Walsh* ~ Venture Capitalist, Bestselling Author, CEO/Founder of Powerteam International

"In a world full of business tactics and strategies, Erik Swanson brings the focus back to where true success begins—the mind. *The Entrepreneurial Mindset* is a must-read for anyone serious about building a thriving business and life."

—*David M. Corbin* ~ 4xWSJ Bestselling Author

"This is the kind of book you highlight, underline, and revisit often. Erik Swanson gives entrepreneurs the mindset tools needed to stay focused, resilient, and unstoppable."

—*Jill Lublin* ~ Bestselling Author, Marketing and Publicity Expert

"Packed with motivation, clarity, and actionable insight, *The Entrepreneurial Mindset* will help you think bigger, act bolder, and build the life you've always envisioned."

—*Paul Blanchard* ~ Executive Coach, Speaker, Bestselling Author

"Entrepreneurs don't just build businesses—they build belief. In *The Entrepreneurial Mindset*, Erik Swanson shows readers how to strengthen their thinking, sharpen their focus, and create unstoppable momentum."

—*(The Real) Ron Swanson*, Erik's Brother, Entrepreneur, Business Development Lead Sustainable H2O Technologies

"As Napoleon Hill teaches in **Think and Grow Rich**, Erik Swanson actively lives and perpetuates the teachings of **The 13 Steps to Riches** by turning true burning desires into accelerated results. I highly recommend **The Entrepreneurial Mindset!**"

—**Jon Kovach Jr.** ~ TEDx Speaker, Bestselling Author, & Mastermind Leader

"What an honor to collaborate with so many personal development leaders from around the world as we Co-Author together honoring the amazing principles by Napoleon Hill in this new book series, **The 13 Steps to Riches**, by Erik "Mr. Awesome" Swanson. Well done, "Mr. Awesome," for putting together such an amazing series. If you want to up-level your life, read every book in this series and learn to apply each of these time-tested steps and principles."

—**Denis Waitley** ~ Author of *Psychology of Winning & The NEW Psychology of Winning—Top Qualities of a 21st Century Winner*

"Just as **Think and Grow Rich** reveals the 13 steps to success discovered by Napoleon Hill after interviewing the richest people around the world (and many who considered themselves failures) in the early 1900s, **The 13 Steps to Riche**s, created and produced by Erik Swanson takes a modern look at those same 13 steps. It brings together many of today's personal development leaders to share their stories of how *The 13 Steps to Riches* have created and propelled their own successes. I am honored to participate and share the power of Faith in my life. If you truly want to accelerate reaching the success you deserve, read every volume of *The 13 Steps to Riches*."

—**Sharon Lechter** ~ 5 Time N.Y. Times Bestselling Author. Author of *Think and Grow Rich for Women*, Co-Author of *Exit Rich, Rich Dad Poor Dad, Three Feet from Gold, Outwitting the Devil* and *Success and Something Greater*

"The most successful book on personal achievement ever written is now being elaborated upon by many of the world's top thought leaders. I'm honored to Co-Author this series on the amazing principles from Napoleon Hill, in *The 13 Steps to Riches*, by Erik "Mr. Awesome" Swanson."

—*Jim Cathcart* ~ Bestselling Author, Certified Speaking Professional (CSP) and Former President of the National Speakers Association (NSA)

"How exciting to team up with the amazing community of leaders such as Erik Swanson, Sharon Lechter, John Assaraf, Denis Waitley and so many more transformational and self-help icons to bring you these timeless and proven concepts in the fields of success and wealth. *The 13 Steps to Riches* book series will help you reach your dreams and accomplish your goals faster than you have ever experienced before!"

—*Dame Marie Diamond* ~ Featured in *The Secret*, Modern-Day Spiritual Teacher, Inspirational Speaker, Feng Shui Master

"If you are looking to crystallize your mightiest dream, rekindle your passion, break through limiting beliefs, and learn from those who have done exactly what you want to do - read this book! In this transformational masterpiece, *The 13 Steps to Riches*, self-development guru Erik Swanson has collected the sage wisdom and time-tested truths from subject matter experts and amalgamated them into a one-stop-shop resource library that will change your life forever!"

—*Dan Clark* ~ Speaker Hall of Fame & N.Y. Times Bestselling Author of *The Art of Significance*

"Life has always been about who you surround yourself with. I am in excellent company with this collaboration from my fellow authors and friends, paying tribute to the life-changing principles by Napoleon Hill in this amazing new book series, *The 13 Steps to Riches*, organized by Habitude Warrior's founder and my dear friend, Erik Swanson. Hill said, 'Your big opportunity may be right where you are now.' This book series is a must-read for anyone who wants to change their lives and prosper, starting now."

—***Alec Stern*** ~ America's Startup Success Expert, Co-Founder of Constant Contact

"Finally, a book series that encompasses the lessons the world needs to learn and apply, but in our modern-day era. As I always teach my students to "Say YES, and then figure out how," I strongly urge you to do the same. Say YES to adding Erik Swanson's ***The 13 Steps to Riches*** book series into your success library and watch both your business as well as your personal life grow as a result."

—***Loral Langemeier*** ~ 5 Time N.Y. Times Bestselling Author, Featured in *The Secret*, Author of *The Millionaire Maker,* and *YES! Energy - The Equation to Do Less, Make More*

"Napoleon Hill had a tremendous impact on my consciousness when I was very young – there were very few books nor the type of trainings that we see today to lead us to success. Whenever you have the opportunity to read and harness ***The 13 Steps to Riches*** as they are presented in this series, be happy (and thankful) that there were many of us out there applying the principles, testing the teachings, making the mistakes, and now being offered to you in a way that they are clear, simple and concise—with samples and distinctions that will make it easier for you to design a successful life which includes adding value to others, solving world problems, and making the world work for 100% of humanity... Read on... those dreams are about to come true!"

—***Dame Doria Cordova*** ~ CEO of Money & You, Excellerated Business School, Global Business Developer, Ambassador of New Education

"Success leaves clues, and the Co-Authors in this awesome book series, ***The 13 Steps to Riches***, will continue the Napoleon Hill legacy with tools, tips, and modern-day principles that greatly expand on the original masterpiece... ***Think and Grow Rich***. If you are serious about living your life to the max, get this book series now!"

—***John Assaraf*** ~ Chairman & CEO NeuroGym, MrNeuroGym.com, N.Y. Times Bestselling author of *Having It All*, *Innercise*, and *The Answer*. Also featured in *The Secret*

"Over the years, I have been blessed with many rare and amazing opportunities to invest my time and energy. These opportunities require a keen eye and immediate action. This is one of those amazing opportunities for you as a reader! I highly recommend you pick up every book in this series of ***The 13 Steps to Riches*** by Habitude Warrior and Erik Swanson! Learn from modern-day leaders who have embraced the lessons from the great Napoleon Hill in his classic book from 1937, ***Think and Grow Rich***."

—***Kevin Harrington*** ~ Original "Shark" on Shark Tank, Creator of the Infomercial, Pioneer of the 'As Seen on TV' brand, Co-Author of *Mentor to Millions*

"When you begin your journey, you will quickly learn of the importance of the first step of ***The 13 Steps To Riches***. A burning desire is the start of all worthwhile achievements. Erik 'Mr. Awesome' Swanson's newest book series contains a wealth of assistance to make your journey both successful and enjoyable. Start today... because tomorrow is not guaranteed on your calendar."

—***Don Green*** ~ 45 Years of Banking, Finance & Entrepreneurship, Bestselling Author of *Everything I Know About Success I Learned From Napoleon Hill* & *Napoleon Hill My Mentor: Timeless Principles to Take Your Success to the Next Level* & *Your Millionaire Mindset*

"A powerful blend of motivation, mindset, and real-world strategy. The Entrepreneurial Mindset belongs on the desk of every entrepreneur and aspiring business leader."

—*Troy Ian Hoffman* ~ Business Architect, Co-Founder of FNDRS.IO

"This book is more than a business guide—it's a message of belief and possibility. Erik Swanson reminds every reader that entrepreneurship is not just about building a business, but about growing into the person you were meant to become."

—*Erin Ley* ~ Bestselling Author, Founder Life on Track

"Erik Swanson has a remarkable ability to speak to the heart of every entrepreneur. **The Entrepreneurial Mindset** is filled with encouragement, wisdom, and the kind of guidance that helps you believe in your dreams again."

—*Cheri Tree*, Bestselling Author, CEO/Founder of B.A.N.K.

"Erik Swanson's message is one of hope, growth, and possibility. This book gently guides entrepreneurs to strengthen their mindset, trust their journey, and keep moving forward even when the road gets tough."

—*Theresa 'TGo' Goss*, Producer, Director, Founder of Squirrel Vision Network

"Reading this book feels like sitting down with a mentor who truly wants the best for you. Erik Swanson's words inspire hope, clarity, and the kind of mindset that helps entrepreneurs rise above fear and step into their true potential."

—*Eric Lofholm,* Master Sales Trainer, Coach, Speaker, Author

# *THE ACTUAL 13 STEPS TO RICHES*

By now, we are positive you have already read, if not once, but multiple times through your life, the original classic book by Napoleon Hill, ***THINK AND GROW RICH.*** If you have not read it yet, go grab a copy today and read a true masterpiece.

We wanted to list, below, the 13 steps Dr. Hill highlights in his book below. We are truly excited to bring a modern-day look at these classic techniques with a 'chicken soup for the soul' feel with all of our celebrity authors' amazing stories.

Step 1:  Decision

Step 2:  Faith

Step 3:  Auto Suggestion

Step 4:  Specialized Knowledge

Step 5:  Imagination

Step 6:  Organized Planning

Step 7:  Decision

Step 8:  Persistence

Step 9:  Mastermind

Step 10: Transmutation

Step 11: Subconscious Mind

Step 12: The Brain

Step 13: Sixth Sense

# ERIK "MR. AWESOME" SWANSON

As an Award-Winning International Keynote Speaker and Multi-Time #1 International Bestselling Author, Erik Swanson is in great demand around the world! He speaks to an average of more than one million people per year. Mr. Swanson has the honor of having been invited to speak to many schools around the world, including the prestigious Harvard University. He is also a recurring faculty member of CEO Space International and an alumni keynote speaker at Vistage Executive Coaching. Mr. Swanson is also the recipient of the 2024 International Book Impact Award and the United States Presidential Lifetime

Achievement Award presented by the White House in 2024 for his ongoing community service and philanthropy work. Erik's speeches can be found on Amazon Prime TV as well as joining the TED Talk Family with his speeches called "A Dose of Awesome" and "NDSO ~ No Drama, Serve Others."

Erik got his start in the self-development world by mentoring directly under Brian Tracy. Quickly climbing to become the top trainer around the world from a group of over 250 handpicked coaches, Erik started to surround himself with the best of the best and very quickly started to be invited to speak on stages alongside such greats as Jim Rohn, Bob Proctor, Les Brown, Sharon Lechter, Jack Canfield, Joe Vitale, Lisa Nichols, and Joe Dispenza—just to name a few. Erik has created and developed the super-popular Habitude Warrior Conferences and Speaker Hearts Mastermind & Retreats, which have a two-year waiting list and include thirty-three top-named speakers from around the world. They are "TED Talk" style events which have quickly climbed to the top ten events not to miss in the United States! He is the creator, founder, and CEO of the Habitude Warrior Mastermind, Global Speakers Mastermind, and Cafe Mastermind. He is also the creator and publisher of many book series such as *The 13 Steps To Riches* book series as well as *The Principles of David & Goliath* book series. His motto is clear: "NDSO!" No Drama – Serve Others!

*www.SpeakerErikSwanson.com*

# *ACKNOWLEDGEMENT TO NAPOLEON HILL*

I would like to personally acknowledge and thank the one and only Napoleon Hill for his work, dedication, and, most importantly, his belief in himself. Whether he realized this or not, his unwavering belief in himself was passed down from generation to generation to millions and millions of individuals across this planet, including me!

I'm sure, at first, as many of us experience throughout our lives as well, he most likely had his doubts. Think about it. Being offered to work for Andrew Carnegie for a full 20 years with zero pay and no guarantee of success had to be a daunting decision. But, I thank you for making that decision years and years ago. It paved the way for countless people who trusted in themselves and found success in their rights. You gave us all hope, desire, and faith to bank on the most important energy in the world—ourselves!

For this, I thank you Sir, from the bottom of my heart and the top of all of our bank accounts. Let us all follow the 13 Steps to Riches and prosper in so many areas of our lives.

~ Erik "Mr. Awesome" Swanson | Multi Time #1 Bestselling Author, TEDx and Harvard Speaker & Student of Napoleon Hill Philosophies

# CONTENTS

*Erik Swanson & Don Green holding the original manuscript of "Outwitting The Devil" by Napoleon Hill*

# *INTRODUCTION BY DON GREEN*

Once you give yourself the gift of reading Erik Swanson's newest book series, *The 13 Steps to Riches*, you are sure to realize why he has earned his nickname, "Mr. Awesome." Readers usually read books for two reasons: they want to be entertained or they want to improve their knowledge in a certain subject. Mr. Awesome's new book series will help you do both.

I urge you to not only read this great book series in it's entirety, but also apply the principles held within into your our life. Use the experience Erik Swanson has gained to reach your own level of success. I highly encourage you to invest in yourself by reading self-help materials, such as The 13 Steps to Riches, and I truly know you will discover that it will be one of the best investments you could ever make.

Don Green
Executive Director and CEO
The Napoleon Hill Foundation

# *FOREWORD BY DR. J.B. HILL*

It was the last time that I would see Napoleon Hill alive. My father had taken his family for a three-day visit to Greenville, South Carolina. My sisters and I were in the back seat of the car, the driver's door was open, and my father was outside saying his goodbyes to his father, my grandfather, Napoleon Hill. Napoleon had three paperback copies of *Think and Grow Rich* in his hands. He leaned into the car and handed a copy to each of us. We quickly discovered a crisp, new ten-dollar bill, which my grandfather had enclosed with his autograph, boldly scrolled in bright green ink at the top of the title page.

He told us that ten dollars was the amount of money a man could earn in a day of hard labor and that we should remember this when we spent our money. He also told us to read his book. Dutifully, I complied, and although I enjoyed his storytelling style, my mind was not mature enough to understand it.

This changed over the course of a dozen years or so. I was lonely and had fallen into the habit of drifting through life. I had no money, no education, and no real skills. By chance, I found and bought a copy of my grandfather's book at a grocery store in North Carolina. This time, I was ready for his book, and, by reading it, I began to understand the value of what Napoleon Hill had placed in my hands. It was a recipe—a thirteen-step recipe for success. All I had to do was follow it—do what my grandfather told me to do. It worked: my life changed.

Many, many people have accomplished the same thing by following Napoleon's thirteen steps to success. One was Joe Dudley, who read *Think and Grow Rich* more than three hundred times. Dudley started life as the son of a tobacco sharecropper in North Carolina. He built a company valued at more than two hundred million dollars by selling products door-to-door. I asked him, "Why? Why would you read that book, any book, so often?" Dudley smiled and told me that reading it keeps his mind straight and that he learns something new with every read.

Bob Proctor read *Think and Grow Rich* every day of his adult life, and many other renowned people also attest to several readings. The most common reason given for this is to gain a deeper understanding of Hill's thinking. However, it is not necessary to read and re-read Hill's book to understand success more fully.

The anthology *The 13 Steps to Riches* does that for us. Each chapter is written by a well-known author with decades of experience reading and thinking about the steps to success. Therefore, *The 13 Steps to Riches* is synergistic in scope and a time-saver for serious students of success. It is certainly worth the read.

# DR. JB HILL

Dr. James Blair Hill, known as Dr. J.B. Hill, was born in Morgantown, West Virginia, to David Hill, the youngest son of Napoleon Hill and Florence Hornor. Dr. Hill's journey embodies dedication, lifelong learning, and a commitment to serve, reflecting the values imparted by his grandfather, renowned author Napoleon Hill.

After graduating high school in 1966, Dr. Hill spent several years at sea on cargo ships. In 1969, he was drafted into the U.S. Marine Corps as a private, beginning a distinguished military career. He later pursued a bachelor's degree in mechanical engineering at Vanderbilt University, graduating in 1973 and earning a commission as a second lieutenant. As a field artillery officer in the Marines, Dr. Hill's discipline and drive led him to further academic achievements, including a Master's degree in Mathematics from the Naval Postgraduate School.

After 26 years of service, Dr. Hill retired from the Marine Corps in 1995. However, his desire to serve took him in a new direction—medicine. At the age of 53, he graduated from medical school, subsequently completing a three-year residency in family medicine. He was board-certified in Family Medicine and earned certifications in Wound Care and Hyperbaric Medicine. Today, he serves as a hospitalist in geriatric care, working to enhance the lives of elderly patients with compassion and expertise. He lives in Bridgeport, West Virginia, with his wife and two children.

Dr. Hill's connection to Napoleon Hill's philosophy was established early when, at the age of 12, his grandfather gifted him a copy of *Think and Grow Rich* with a simple yet profound directive: "Read it." Yet it wasn't until he was 23 that Dr. Hill grasped the full impact of his grandfather's teachings. This understanding became a cornerstone of his life, guiding him through challenges and instilling a sense of purpose that has defined his legacy in both his military and medical careers.

Through his life and work, Dr. Hill exemplifies the timeless principles of personal empowerment and service, leaving his own mark on a legacy that spans generations.

*www.NapHill.org*

# CHAPTER 1

# DESIRE IS A LIFE'S JOURNEY

The late, great Dr. Napoleon Hill wrote in his amazing masterpiece from 1937, *Think and Grow Rich*, that desire is the starting point of all achievement! I 1,000 percent agree with him. I would take it one step further and say that desire is and should be included in the journey, as well as the finish line, of all achievement, and you should even allow it to catapult you to the next desire, to up-level you as an awesome human being on this planet! What an absolute honor it is to be able to learn and follow in the steps of such leaders in my journey in the world of personal development.

My definition of desire has changed over the many years from when I started tapping into it about twenty-four years ago. At first, I believed desire was all about what I wanted to accomplish. For me, it was an internal dialogue that included only myself. It consisted of the accomplishments of my personal goals in life. Although utilizing desire is a fantastic way to improve my personal life, I soon started to see that it was not all about me. Now, my true definition of desire is one that helps the world and everyone around me. It's a burning, internal, awesome, goal strategy with a commitment to never give up on my mission to assist people around me to up-level their lives for the better. Life is a team sport. Let's get in this game together.

Desire shows up in so many areas of our lives. I recall the very first time I had a glimpse of the concept of desire. It included seven letters, starting with the letter "k," and ending with my five-year-old heart pounding. It was my first day of kindergarten. She walked by me as we were putting our little lunch boxes in the cubby holes. Her name was Kirsten! Wow! I was in love! She had such long, golden hair, like an angel, and a smile to match. I'm not sure if she noticed that every few days, I would sit closer and closer to her until I was finally right next to her in class. Ahhhh, heaven! I finally made it. Now, I just need to muster up enough courage to speak to her. Oops, nap-time already? Okay, well, I guess I'll strike up a conversation after we take a little nap together.

Now, I would love to tell you that the conversation went very smoothly.

You know, "So, what's an angel like you doing in kindergarten?" … or like some cool line like that I threw her way. Nope. That wasn't the case.

I think my very first words to her were something like, "Your choice of crayon color is impeccable." She smiled and just walked away.

Okay, I vow to myself from here on out, I will kiss this beautiful angel, Kirsten, by the end of the school year. I'm committed! Nothing is going to get in my way… not even me. It's my very first desire and goal that I remember setting for myself as a little human being.

Fast-forward to my senior year of high school. When every one of my friends knew where they were going to go to college the following year, I still struggled with my decision. Or, should I say that my grades helped me struggle with the decision? I was so determined to go to the same university that all of my friends were going to, yet, my grades were determined to place me elsewhere.

As I was pondering what to do, my best friend in school suggested that I become friends with one of the jocks in my high school, simply because his father was the actual dean of the university I was desiring to attend.

Okay, mission set! Desire on! I'm ready. Now what? I didn't technically have a plan of action. But, what I did have was the burning desire to never quit, and I innately realized that what's "inside of me" would determine what's "in my outside reality." Dr. Napoleon Hill teaches us that "Desire outwits Mother Nature" and to have a "Definite of Purpose." I decided to use these principles and GO FOR IT, NO MATTER WHAT! *I mean, what do I have to lose?* I thought.

 So, off I went to find this jock and become friends with him. It worked! I simply found common ground with him in something he was interested in. That interest turned out to be downhill skiing. Great… I'm *not* a skier. But, I'll tell you what. I was a skier for as long as it took to win his friendship over. It worked!

Because of my tenacity and determination to complete my current mission of desire, I got accepted to my school of choice and went to the university with all my friends. Of course, with a little—or should I say a lot—of help from my new jock friend and his pull with his father. Never allow yourself to give up on yourself! You deserve greatness, and greatness is simply on the other side of your determination, commitment, and action to your goals and desires.

After university and a few years of trying to figure out what I wanted to do with my life, I was introduced to a brilliant mind. He was apparently very well-known as one of the main leaders on the planet for personal development, sales, and management training. After I asked around and started to hear his name over and over again from those I admired in very successful businesses, I started to set a goal to work with him. Not only work with him, but become one of his very best trainers. Not only become one of his best trainers, but actually share stages with him around the world. This man I'm referring to is the one and only Brian Tracy!

Would you like to know a secret? If you ever desire to work with someone who is brilliant, but who you feel is untouchable and out of reach to you, start studying his or her work. Start applying his or her work and teachings into your everyday habits. Start surrounding yourself with his or her thoughts, and soon, the Universe will reward you for your burning desire! This is exactly what I did. I figured that if I could positively "brainwash" myself with all of Brian Tracy's great teachings and habits, then I could become someone like him and ultimately reach the success he did.

In one of my other books, *Crush and Dominate*, I teach a concept called "Copy, Don't Copy." It's simply the concept of training yourself to think, act, and grow like the mentors you desire to be like, but still being authentically you. You can use this concept in any area of your life. It doesn't have to be just in business. Ultimately, I became an International Senior Trainer with my mentor, Brian Tracy, and traveled the world working with him for about ten years. This changed my life! Or should I say, "I changed my life!" You can, too. You simply need to make that commitment and realize that nothing is out of your reach, as long as you believe in the concept of having a "burning desire."

Looking back at the journey of my life as it pertains to how important this concept of desire truly is, I would have to say that although I was utilizing the concept, I never fully understood the true meaning. Yes, I conquered tons of goals that I thought were part of my own burning desires. But, as I mentioned at the beginning of this conversation, I have come to realize lately that it's not all about ourselves. A true "burning desire" to me is all about helping the world and everyone on this planet.

Take, for example, this book series. I could have easily written all of these chapters by myself about my journey and how I grew from each of the 13 Steps to Riches. But, it's *not* all about me. It's about how "WE" as a collective group of *awesome* individuals make up an amazing team to go further by helping each other grow. This is how we, as a team, can help others grow as well. This series you are about to embark upon— and hopefully, embrace—will give you a modern-day's journey from people from around the world who use these amazing 13 Steps to Riches principles in their lives, while dealing with struggles, adversities, and triumphs. This is "OUR" journey together. I truly hope you enjoy it and join us!

Oh, and if you are still wondering if I ever ended up kissing my kindergarten crush, Kirsten, you will simply have to read this next chapter to find out. I may have even married her!

*DENIS WAITLEY*

# MOTIVATION BY DESIRE

Positive self-motivation is the inner drive that keeps you moving forward in pursuit of your goals. Winners in every field in the game of life are driven by desire. There never has been a consistent winner in any profession who didn't have that burning desire to win… internalized. Although the Scriptures have preached it as a basic axiom in life for centuries, this concept was first presented in the self-improvement industry by Earl Nightingale in his platinum audio recording of "The Strangest Secret." The strangest secret is that we become what we think about most of the time. In other words, we and our children are motivated every day and moved by our current dominant thoughts. We are moved in the direction of what we dwell on. We can't concentrate on the reverse of an idea. Everyone in life is self-motivated, positively or negatively. Even a decision to do nothing is a decision based on motivation.

In the field of psychology, we make a basic distinction between intrinsic and extrinsic motivation. Having intrinsic motivation means doing something for its own sake., like playing a sport just for the joy of playing. On the other hand, extrinsic motivation pulls you by the power of some external benefit or tangible reward you'll attain by taking action, as in the case of a professional athlete who plays primarily for money rather than for the fun or challenge of the sport. It also influences people in their business careers, especially among those who are driven fundamentally by the income they receive rather than by the love of the service they provide.

Motivation is a highly emotional state and the great physical and mental motivators in life such as survival and love are filled with emotion. And the two key emotions which dominate all human motivation, with opposite, but nearly equally effective results, are fear and desire. Fear, of course, is the most powerful, negative motivator of all. Fear is the great dictator, that forces us to do things that we feel we have to do because of the consequences. Fear is the great inhibitor, the red light that tells us that we can't do things, because of the obstacles and risks.

Through the years I've been telling the story of a man who may unwittingly have become a victim of his own negative premonition, a kind of self-inflicted voodoo spell. It was a true account of a man named, Nick Sitzman, a strong, healthy individual who worked as a yardman for a railroad company in Omaha, Nebraska. According to his supervisor, Nick was a good worker who got along fine with his fellow workers and was reliable on the job. He had one noticeable fault, however. He was a notorious worrier. He was cynical about everything and usually feared the worst about the world situation, the economy, the weather and the future, in general.

One summer day, the train crews were informed that they could quit an hour early in honor of the foreman's birthday.

Accidentally, Nick was locked in an empty, isolated refrigerator boxcar, in which he had been working, that was in the yard for repairs, and the rest of the workmen left the site. Nick panicked. He banged and shouted until his fists were raw and his voice hoarse. No one paid any attention. If they heard him, they associated the sound with a playground nearby or with the noise of other trains backing in and out of the yard.

"Hey, let me out of here, it must be zero degrees in this refrigerator car," he must have thought. "If I can't get out soon, I'll freeze to death." He found a cardboard box and, shivering uncontrollably, he scrawled this message to his wife and family: "So cold, body is getting numb. If I could just go to sleep. These may be my last words."

The next morning, the crew slid open the heavy doors of the boxcar and found Nick dead. An autopsy revealed that every physical sign in his body indicated he had frozen to death. But the irony was that the refrigeration unit was inoperative and there was plenty of fresh air in the boxcar. It was a mild summer afternoon and evening, with the temperature inside steady at about sixty-one degrees. His fear motivation became a self-fulfilling prophecy.

As a positive power, belief becomes the promise of the realization of things hoped for and unseen. As a negative power, it is the premonition of our deepest fears and unseen darkness. A self-fulfilling prophecy perhaps can be best defined as a statement or concept that is not necessarily true nor false, but is capable of becoming true if it is believed and internalized.

Desire is like a strong, positive magnet. It beckons and welcomes us toward our goals. Fear usually looks through the rear view mirror at missed opportunities and problems and with apprehension to the future.

Fear breeds compulsion. Desire creates positive propulsion. Fear breeds inhibition. Desire triggers ignition power. Winners have learned how to concentrate on the desired results, rather than possible problems. And winners dwell on the rewards of success, instead of the penalties of failure.

## THE LAW OF ATTRACTION TAKES ACTION

Over a decade ago, I participated in the video and book project called "The Secret", based upon the Law of Attraction. One way or another, our actions cause rewards and consequences. "To every action," as Sir Isaac Newton observed, "there is always opposed an equal reaction." Good begets good and evil leads to more evil. This is one of the universe's eternal, fundamental truths which I have referred to as The Unfailing Boomerang or the Law of Cause and Effect.

It means that every cause (action) will create an effect (reaction) approximately equal in intensity. Making good use of our minds, skills, and talents will bring positive rewards in our outer lives. Assuming the personal responsibility to make the best use of our talents and time will result in an enormous gain in happiness, success, and wealth. This is true of everyone.

The truly successful winners, those who have built financial empires or accomplished great deeds for society, are those who have taken personal responsibility to heart and to soul. By being true to themselves and others, they achieve success, wealth, and inner happiness. In the end, we ourselves--far more than any outsider--are the people with the greatest ability to steal our own time, talents, and accomplishments.

I'm fond of a story from the Old Testament Book of Leviticus about a sacred ceremony called "The Escaped Goat." When the people's troubles became overwhelming in those early days, a healthy male goat was led into the temple. The tribe's highest priest placed his hand on the animal's head and solemnly recited the long list of the people's woes. Then the goat was released--and it ran off, supposedly taking the human troubles and evil spirits with him. That was some four thousand years ago, but the concept of the scapegoat remains in full force today. Blaming someone else or something else for our problems is nearly as old as civilization--and stays consistently young. When Adam ate of the apple, he quickly pointed at Eve. "The woman you've put here with me made me do it," he said.

We live in a land of incredible abundance. Americans enjoy material riches and a civic and legal inheritance that people of other countries continue to die for. We protest for individual liberty and social order in the same breath. We strive for material wealth, hoping that spiritual riches will come with it as a bonus. We plead for more protection from crime but demand less interference in our social habits. We want to cut taxes and build our own empires--at the same time, we want our government to provide more financial security. But we can't have it both ways. If we want results, we must pay the price.

Life's greatest risk is depending on others for your security, which can really come only by planning, acting, and making choices that will make you independent.

> *There was a very cautious man,*
> *Who never laughed or played;*
> *He never risked, he never tried,*
> *He never sang or prayed.*
> *And when he one day passed away,*
> *His insurance was denied;*
> *For since he really never lived,*
> *They claimed he never died.*

There are two primary choices in our lives: to accept conditions as they exist or to assume the responsibility for changing them. The price of success includes taking responsibility for giving up bad habits and invalid assumptions; setting a worthy example in our own lives; leading ourselves and others down a new and unfamiliar path; working more to reach a goal and being willing to delay gratification along the way; distancing ourselves from a peer group that isn't helping us succeed and therefore tends or wants to hold us back; and being willing to face criticism and jealousy from people who would like to keep us stuck in place with them.

My decades of research have convinced me that the happiest, best-adjusted individuals in their present and older lives are those who believe they have a strong measure of control over their lives. They seem to choose more appropriate responses to what occurs and to stand up to inevitable changes with less apprehension. They learn from their past mistakes, rather than replay them. They spend time "doing" in the present, rather than fearing what may happen. So, stop stewing and start doing. If the pandemic has taught us anything, it is that we must b prepared for sudden change and surprises on a daily basis. Being resilient in turbulent times is our new reality.

## ACTION TNT: TODAY NOT TOMORROW

My grandfather owned a bookstore and bindery in San Diego where I used to work on weekends as a pre-teen and teenager. In addition to gluing books together and sweeping out his store, I loved browsing and sampling the stacks of books on the shelves. It was like a candy store of wisdom to me. He had a poster on the wall that I copied in my notebook because my grandpa said it was an important lesson for me to learn when I was young. He said procrastination is a favorite hiding place for people who are afraid to risk making mistakes, which is why he almost never put off any important decisions regarding the family. I have memorized that poster and refer to it often when I spend time puttering, majoring in minors and doing meaningless activities that are tension-relieving instead of goal achieving. The title is simply—Tomorrow:

He was going to be what he wanted to be—tomorrow. None would be kinder and braver than he—tomorrow. A friend who was troubled and weary he knew, who'd be glad for a lift and needed it too, on him he would call and see what he could do – tomorrow. Each morning he'd stack up the letters he'd write— tomorrow. And thought of the clients he'd fill with delight— tomorrow. But he hadn't a minute to stop on his way, "More time I will give to others," he'd say—"tomorrow." The greatest of leaders this man would have been—tomorrow. The world would have hailed him had he ever seen—tomorrow. But in fact, he passed on, and he faded from view. And all that he left here when his life was through, was a mountain of things he intended to do—TOMORROW.

## MOTIVATION INTO MOTIVE-ACTION

Here are some motivation actions you can take to reach your goals instead of letting fear and negativity keep you in a constant state of frustration and anxiety:

1. Remember: we become what we think about. What the mind harbors, the body manifests in some way. Focus your mind, which I call your software program) on your desired goals that you want your brain and body (your hard-drive and hardware) to achieve.

2. View failure as target correction. Failure is only a detour, not a dead end. The person interested in success has to learn to view failure as a healthy, inevitable part of the process of getting to the top. I look at failure as the fertilizer of success. Don't roll in it. Use the experience as growth material. So make a pact with yourself. I suggest you write an agreement with yourself. Promise that you won't allow a failure to be more than a learning experience that allows you to move more quickly to the place you want to be.

3. Keep your self-talk affirmative. Whether you're at work, at home or on the golf course or tennis court, your subconscious is recording every word. Instead of "should have" say "will do." Instead of "if only" say "next time." Instead of "Yes, but" say "Why not?" Instead of "problem" say "opportunity." Instead of "difficult" say "challenging." "Instead of "could have" say "My goal." Instead of "Someday" say "Today." Say "In the hole, before you putt on the green while playing golf, and "First serve in" when it's your serve on the tennis court.

4. Forget perfection. Only the saints are perfect—and "Sainthood is acceptable only in saints." Accept the flaws and count your blessings instead of your blemishes.

5. Declare a moratorium on negatives—negative thoughts, negative people, negative forms of entertainment. Keep your desire to succeed strong by erasing thoughts of the downside. To win you must continuously motivate yourself toward your goals. And you must be willing to do this yourself.

6. Be willing to say to yourself, "I'm on the right road. I'm doing OK. I'm succeeding." We too frequently become adept at identifying our flaws and failures. Become equally adept at recognizing your achievements. What are you doing now that you weren't doing one month ago … six months ago … a year ago. What habits have changed? Chart your progress.

Doing well once or twice is relatively easy. Real winning is continuously moving ahead. Winning is tough, in part, because it is so easy to revert to old habits and former lifestyles. Over the long run, you need to give yourself regular feedback and monitor your performance. Reinforce yourself positively to stay on track. Don't wait for an award ceremony, promotion, friend or mentor to show appreciation for your work. Do it yourself! Do it now. Take pride in your own efforts on a daily basis.

7. Set up a dynamic daily routine. Getting into a positive routine or groove, instead of a negative rut, will help you become more effective. Why is the subway the most energy efficient means of transportation? Because it runs on a track. Think of the order in your day, instead of the routine. Don't worry about sameness, neatness or everything exactly in its place. Order is being able to do what you really choose and not taking on more than you can manage. Order frees you up. Get into the swing of a healthy, daily routine and discover how much more control you'll gain in your life.

Here are 5 keys to adding order to a winning routine:

Simplify – challenge complicated plans or processes.

Don't spend a lot of time searching for things – you probably don't need them anyway.

Do what you promise to do – and promise only what you can do.

Set effective agendas with others ahead of time – so neither of you is disappointed.

Monitor yourself in order to make sure you accomplish what you set out to do.

And remember:

Change your attitude and lifestyle, and many of your outcomes will change automatically. Because you are an uncut gemstone of priceless value. Cut and polish your potential with knowledge, skills and service and you will be in great demand throughout your life. Optimists rule the future. Imagination and innovation flourish when nations, companies, teams, families and individuals are motivated by the rewards of success, instead of the penalties of failure. Fear compels and inhibits. Desire is that burning fire of hope within that turns dreams into reality. Ask any athlete training for 1200 days for an opportunity to be an Olympian, what motivates her or him. It is the torch of passion.

# DR. DENIS WAITLEY

Denis Waitley has inspired, informed, challenged, and entertained audiences for over 25 years, from the boardrooms of multi-national corporations to the locker rooms of world-class athletes and in the meeting rooms of thousands of conventioneers throughout the world. Recently, he was voted business speaker of the year by the Sales and Marketing Executives Association and by Toastmasters International and inducted into the International Speakers Hall of Fame.

With over 10 million audio programs sold in 14 languages, Denis Waitley is one of the most listened-to voices on personal and career success. He is the author of 16 non-fiction books, including several International bestsellers, *Seeds of Greatness*, *Being the Best*, *The Winners' Edge*, *The Joy of Working*, and *Empire of the Mind*.

His audio album, *The Psychology of Winning*, is the all-time bestselling program on self-mastery.

Denis Waitley has studied and counseled winners in every field, from Apollo astronauts to Super Bowl champions, from sales achievers to government leaders and youth groups.

During the 1980s, he served as Chairman of Psychology on the U.S. Olympic Committee's Sports Medicine Council, responsible for the performance enhancement of all U.S. Olympic athletes.

Denis Waitley is a founding director of the National Council on Self-Esteem and the President's Council on Vocational Education, and recently received the "Youth Flame Award" from the National Council on Youth Leadership for his outstanding contribution to high school youth leadership.

As President of the International Society for Advanced Education, inspired by Dr. Jonea Salk, he counseled returning POWs from Vietnam and conducted simulation and stress management seminars for Apollo astronauts.

***www.DenisWaitley.com***

# CHAPTER 2

# FAITH REMOVES LIMITATIONS AND OPENS UP OUR WORLD

The late, great Napoleon Hill once wrote, "Riches begin in the form of thought! The amount is limited only by the person in whose mind the thought is put into motion. Faith removes limitations!"

What is Faith? Where does Faith come from? How do we sustain Faith in our lives?

I believe that Faith is an 'all-knowing' entity that lives deep in our souls. It is what I also refer to as our "Internal Belief System," or "IBS." We all have an internal belief system in which we call upon each and every day. We may not actually notice or realize we are calling upon it. But we are. Have you ever noticed yourself actually talking to yourself, maybe not out loud, but under our breath or even quietly in our heads? And, you actually answer yourself as well in that same fashion. *That* is the voice of Faith!

When I was traveling to speak on various stages throughout the world and sharing the stage with the one and only Jim Rohn, I recall he and I sitting down from time to time, having deep philosophical conversations.

One of those conversations with Mr. Rohn was focused around Faith and our belief systems. He shared with me that he believed all of the 'answers' were all already inside of us. I asked him, "What do you mean?" He replied, "I believe that we all simply need to adjust our thinking patterns. Rather than searching 'outside' of us, we should be searching 'inside' of us." He explained that he believed God ensured all of the answers we seek deep inside of each and every one of us! The goal is to search internally, rather than externally, and we shall all find the answers we truly seek.

But the issue most people around the world have is that they are always seeking and searching for answers externally! The grass always seems to be greener across the street! This mindset is detrimental to the success of those individuals. It's time for people to have Faith in themselves, knowing that our higher source has given each of us the tools to excel in our lives beyond our wildest and amazing dreams. In fact, the world and planet grows in such a positive way as one community and entity when everyone is in alignment with this mindset theory.

Have you ever heard of the saying: "If you want to go fast, go alone. If you want to go far, go with a team!?" Once we all, as a community, vow to be in alignment with the Faith mindset or

"IBS," a movement starts to form! It is so powerful and vital for our world as a whole. And it all starts with Faith!

Think of a team; for instance, a football team. Once you have the alignment of the Faith mindset embodied not only in the minds, but also in the souls of each and every player on the team, you start to form a community that is unstoppable. And, on the flip side of that coin, once you allow a "bad apple" mindset to spread within the community, or in this case the football team… it starts to corrupt the other team members' mindsets. This negative mindset or non-faith mindset will slowly and ultimately bring down the rest of the team or community unless two things happen: 1) You change the negative individual's mindset into the positive mindset embodied by the other members of the community. 2) You extract or cut the negative "bad apple" individual out of the group or community.

This concept shows up in many areas of our lives. Yet, most people never make those decisions to actually do one of those two actions. Most people simply hope things will change. You can't change the people around you, but you can change the people around you! Let me be one to tell you the simple truth in that most people never change. It's what my mentor, Brian Tracy, would always tell me in that people show you their true colors if you actually pay attention. So, pay attention! Success leaves clues - so does failure.

Your goal should be to seek out or build communities in which the Faith alignment mindset will be prevalent, consistent, and sustainable. This is what I set out to do once I had my "satori" moment. A satori moment is what you have an awakening… or what the Japanese call "instant enlightenment." Years ago, I never really considered the fact that who I was surrounding myself with made a difference in my success equation. It does! Now, and for the past 10 years, I have been extremely conscious and aware of who I allow to be in my space, community, businesses, and even personal world. I only seek out those who have the Faith mindset.

So, where does this Faith mindset ultimately come from? It's easy, it comes from within! It's like I said before… It's a knowing, it's a belief system, and it's an understanding of yourself through your higher source. Give yourself permission to allow it into your life. Give yourself permission to enjoy the success benefits in which having Faith will give to you.

I recall many of my friends throughout the years commenting to me that they love the fact that I always seem to have an abundance mindset. They see that I always have a calmness about me and a knowing that things will always work out. It truly comes from having Faith! I believe having Faith in yourself is absolutely vital. I believe our higher source gave all of us this ability to tap into Faith at any given moment of the day. In fact, once you truly master the art of tapping into your Faith, you start to experience what I call the "Ultimate Belief System," or "UBS." It is a *knowing* that it will all work out for the best. Having "UBS" is so powerful as you start to turn it on more and more throughout the day. Your decisions tend to get easier and always seem to land in the success field rather than the failure field.    This is how you sustain your Faith... by continuing to use it daily. Consistency is key!

As Napoleon Hill explained to us early on, Faith removes limitations; it truly does! Whenever I tap into my "UBS," I start to notice that success started to flow towards me rather than away. Once I started seeing this on a regular basis, I started to test it out. I would consciously be aware of the outcome when I chose different decisions...especially when there was a fork in the road. You know those for kin the road decisions when you feel the pressure of making a right or wrong decision? Those can be brutal. But I decided to tap into my "UBS" mindset and track the outcomes. Wow, the results were amazing! I actually found out that I was making the *right* decisions at about a 90% rate! It was crazy, I thought! But I kept on testing this theory and guess what happened? 90% is what kept on happening! Ok, I'm on to something here. Ladies and gentlemen, Faith and my "UBS" theory is here to stay. I'm sold on it now!

I suggest you give it a go as well in your life. You literally have nothing to lose by incorporating Faith into your daily habits. It's truly one of my habitudes now and is here to stay forever.

Oh, and if you are still wondering if I ever ended up kissing my kindergarten crush, Kirsten, well, I can't tell you that yet. But what I can tell you is that I had so much Faith that she would at least accompany me to the school-ground swing sets during at least one of the recess breaks coming up. I mean, if I didn't believe in myself or have Faith, then I was doomed to succeed right from the start. So, what do I have to lose? Absolutely nothing! Onwards to ask Kirsten to walk with me and swing on the playground swing sets. Ugh, I'm so nervous to ask her. But I reminded myself that she may be nervous as well. And heck, maybe she won't notice that I'm so nervous. Hmmm, fat chance for that, mainly because of the sweat pouring down my face and my sweaty palms. Ok, new plan, don't let her touch my hands cause that would be a sure giveaway. Ok, here goes! Wish me luck… or better yet, wish me Faith!

*SHARON LECHTER*

# HAVE YOU ADDED VALUE INTO SOMEONE'S LIFE TODAY?

What role has FAITH played in your life and in your success? Try to remember a time when you "powered through" a difficult period in your life. How did FAITH show up and help you through?

When I asked myself this question, I first think about the spiritual aspect of faith and my trust in a higher power… but I also think about the faith I have in myself. It reminds me of my father and a simple question he would ask me each night.

## "HAVE YOU ADDED VALUE TO SOMEONE'S LIFE TODAY?"

My dad used to ask me that question every night when I was growing up. He has been gone for 15 years, but I still ask myself this same question every evening.

As a child, I didn't understand how dramatically this simple question would impact my life. By concentrating on adding value to others' lives, you don't focus on just yourself or your personal desires. But even more importantly, when you see the positive impact your actions make in the lives of others, it makes you feel better about yourself. It builds your self-confidence, or faith in yourself by helping others find faith in themselves. That is truly adding value to the world.

When most people hear the word faith, they think of faith from a spiritual perspective. Spiritual faith in God or a higher power is incredibly important and creates a fundamental belief system that shapes who we are and who we become as adults.

It is also important not to neglect the faith that we can build in ourselves and in each other every single day through the thoughts, words and actions that we choose. I realize that the nightly question from my father and my desire to help others helped me build faith and self-confidence as a result of my service to others.

In addition to spiritual faith and faith in yourself you can have faith in others, faith in your endeavors and faith that you will succeed.

## WHAT IS THE FIRST THOUGHT THE WORD FAITH TRIGGERS IN YOUR MIND?

Many of history's greatest thought leaders have highlighted the importance of faith.

*Faith consists in believing when it is beyond the power of reason to believe.*
~ Voltaire

*He who has faith has... an inward reservoir of courage, hope, confidence, calmness, and assuring trust that all will come out well—even though to the world it may appear to come out most badly.* B. C. Forbes (founder of Forbes Magazine)

*Faith is the strength by which a shattered world shall emerge into the light.*
~ Helen Keller

*When you focus on being a blessing, God makes sure that you are always blessed in abundance.*
~ Joel Osteen

*In faith there is enough light for those who want to believe and enough shadows to blind those who don't.*
~ Blaise Pascal

*Keep your dreams alive. Understand to achieve anything requires faith and belief in yourself, vision, hard work, determination, and dedication. Remember all things are possible for those who believe.*
~ Gail Devers

In *Think and Grow Rich*, Napoleon Hill himself challenged the notion that faith is only about religious belief. Faith becomes the beacon of light that provides a path forward and engages your subconscious mind. Without faith, negativity fills your subconscious and multiplies more negativity. On the other hand, optimism, positivity, and faith create the foundation that shields your mind from negativity and from which success can be built.

Let's review Hill's definition of FAITH and the role it plays in creating success in your life:

## HAVE FAITH IN YOURSELF: FAITH IN THE INFINITE

*FAITH is the "external elixir" which gives life, power, and action to the impulse of thought!*
*FAITH is the starting point of all accumulation of riches!*
*FAITH is the basis of all "miracles" and all mysteries which cannot be analyzed by the rules of science!*
*FAITH is the only known antidote for FAILURE!*
*FAITH is the element, the "chemical" which, when mixed with prayer, gives one direct communication with Infinite Intelligence.*
*FAITH is the element which transforms the ordinary vibration of thought, created by the finite mind of man, into the spiritual equivalent.*
*FAITH is the only agency through which the cosmic force of Infinite Intelligence can be harnessed and used by man.*

The importance of faith became very clear to me during the writing process for *Three Feet From Gold*, my first *Think and Grow Rich* series book with the Napoleon Hill Foundation co-authored with Greg Reid. As we interviewed successful business men and women, we found they shared common traits that drove them to success. But even more importantly we found the common attributes that helped them drive and persevere through the tough times.. turning obstacles they faced into opportunities. As a result of our research we formulated the Personal Success Equation to share the common elements of their success stories.

It is as follows:

[ ( P + T ) x A x A ] + F = Personal Success Equation
[( **Passion** + **Talent** ) x **Association** x **Action** ] + **F**aith = Personal Success Equation

Just as Hill discovered the principles of success by research and study of the most successful people of his time and shared them in *Think and Grow Rich*, the personal success equation was derived by analysis of what was key to the success of modern industry leaders and their ability to overcome obstacles. When you combine your **Passion** and your **Talent** with the right **Association**s and then take the right **Action**s you are well on your way to success. Your Passion and Talents are personal to you, often learned in school or from life experience. But true success is achieved through the Power of Association and taking action towards your goals. And we almost went to print with *Three Feet From Gold* with that as the formula but I recognized that a huge common element with these industry leaders that was missing was their incredible Faith. Faith in themselves, faith in what they were doing, faith that it was needed and necessary and faith that they would succeed. That faith kept them moving and persevering even during tough times when others would have easily quit "three feet from gold!"

In addition, we discovered that for many business owners that "F" actually stood for Fear, not Faith. And it was that Fear that make it easy for them to give up and quit, choosing NOT to persevere. This fear prevented them from achieving the success they deserved.

It is impossible to have Faith and Fear in your mind at the same time. Having faith helps you keep fear under control. Fear does one of two things - it paralyzes us or motivates us. The vast majority of us are paralyzed by fear so we fail to take action. We hide away and isolate and end up missing opportunities that are right there in front of us. This fear stops us and keeps us from moving past the obstacle that caused the fear.

When we internalize that fear it becomes destructive. We start thinking things like, "I am not good enough, I am not qualified, I am not thin enough, I am just not as lucky as he is." In each of these statements we are giving up our own power and judging ourselves through the eyes of others. This negativity eats away at our self-confidence and destroys our faith in ourselves. If we can learn to identify the fear and turn it into energy and action, we can overcome it, stand tall in our own power and place ourselves in the position of greatest potential.

Hill provides us with a roadmap to overcome fear in *Outwitting the Devil*, which he actually wrote in 1938, intending it to be the sequel to *Think and Grow Rich*. But it was kept in a vault until I had to honor to annotate it and share it in 2015. (Why was it kept in the vault? His wife was afraid of the title!) In this manuscript, Hill provides incredible insights into why we hold ourselves back and fail to reach the level of success we deserve. He takes on every taboo of our times... sex, politics, education, religion, diet, alcohol, cigarettes just to name a few… and shares how fear manipulates us in each one of these areas and prevents us from achieving the success we deserve.

This fear robs us of the ability to think for ourselves. To have control over our own thoughts. He talks about fear of poverty, fear of death, fear of criticism, fear of old age, fear of loss of love. I believe the fear of criticism is pervasive in society today and prevents us from finding our own voice. We are so afraid of what others will think of us, of being embarrassed or being different that we "go with the flow" and don't carve our own path.

*Outwitting the Devil* shows you how to break the paralysis of fear and take control of your thoughts, your actions and your results. It all starts with Definiteness of Purpose. When you know what your definiteness of purpose is, it gives you courage and energy to move forward. Just as asking myself if I have added value to someone's life today does, it takes you out of yourself and allows you to focus on being of contribution to the world.

In fact, every successful business defines its definiteness of purpose by the problem it solves or the need that it serves. It is the mission of the business. As an individual you should also incorporate your personal mission statement that allows you to stay focused your definiteness of purpose.

The next step is Mastery over Self which is creating the self-discipline that creates positive habits that allow you to keep focused and demonstrates that you truly are in control of your thoughts and actions.

But in his wisdom, Hill also recognized that we all make mistakes, so we need to acknowledge them and learn from them. Too often when we make mistakes, instead of learning from them, we carry them around with us like heavy baggage defining ourselves as failures. It is important to understand that mistakes happen to all of us and when they do it is important to ask yourself what the lesson is…so you don't repeat the mistake. *It is important to remember that mistakes are occurrences…not definitions.*

But Hill also recognized that even the strongest faith can be tested by everyday life. He shared the importance of controlling our environment. What are you listening to? What are you reading? Who are you spending time with? Who are you listening to? Just imagine entering a room that is full of people crying at the funeral of a child…do you feel the emotional pull of sadness? Now imagine entering a room of people singing and dancing…where you immediately smile and feel the beat of the music. That small example demonstrates the impact of our environment on our attitude and emotional well-being.

It is very important to surround yourself with people who support you and want you to succeed. And it is even more important to limit your exposure to people who try to hold you back or pull you down. Environment includes what you and those around you feed your subconscious. In *Think and Grow Rich*, Hill shares the importance of Autosuggestion, feeding your mind and subconscious with positive messaging to bolster your outlook, your confidence and faith in yourself. It not only helps nurture your faith but gives you energy and motivation to move forward toward accomplishing your definiteness of purpose. When the pandemic stopped us in our tracks, I was distressed by all the negative messaging and the amount of fear and hopelessness it was generating. I took action and started sharing a daily message of hope and positivity, called daily ATMs (Abundance, Tips and Mentorship). The ATMs are an autosuggestion tool for you if you are looking for positive messaging and environment. I end each message every day with the same exercise. I ask you to repeat in the mirror, "I am fabulous!" And then I respond, "Yes you are!" (*atm.sharonlechter.com*)

Going hand in hand with controlling your environment, and equally as important is controlling your time. So often we know what we need to do...we just don't do it! (Are you feeling busted right now?) It could be fear that is holding you back or a lack of motivation. Start by analyzing your calendar. Are you spending time...or are you investing time? You can make money, lose it, and make it back. But time is your only truly precious resource. Once it is gone...you don't get it back. Commit to investing your time in the pursuit of your Definiteness of Purpose and you will feel the faith and confidence in yourself grow.

When I start working with new clients, I carefully review the Personal Success Equation with them. Entrepreneurship can be very lonely because entrepreneurs are trying to do everything themselves relying solely on their own passion and talent. This comes from being taught to work alone in school. But business is a team sport and collaboration is essential for innovation and success. While my clients are strong in their passion and talents, the areas that are often weakest for them in their Personal Success Equations are usually the Associations they have as well as the lack of Faith in themselves.

After years of mentoring clients, I can honestly say having the right Associations are the best and quickest way to build your Faith and confidence in yourself. Those new associations can include having the right mentor, people on your team who are strong where you are weak, the right advisors, and the right industry collaborators. When you have the right people around you and you have a bad day, they step up to bolster you and keep you focused on the big picture. They help transform your fear into faith. Having the team moving together toward your definiteness of purpose is much more fun and rewarding that trying to do it all alone.

To ensure you truly succeed and overcome any obstacles that may stand in your way, you definitely need the right association and faith. Having faith in yourself, your mission and your ability to succeed, will help you persevere when times are difficult and propel you to even greater heights of success.

When I wrote *Think and Grow Rich for Women*, I asked Sara O'Meara and Yvonne Fedderson to share their thoughts on Faith and I was so impressed with what they shared that I am including it here as well. Sara and Yvonne are the founders of Childhelp, the largest non-profit dedicated to the prevention and treatment of child abuse saving over 11 million children from the horrors of abuse. (*www.childhelp.org*) They have been nominated for the Nobel Peace Prize ten times. They are dear friends, mentors of mine, and true angels on earth. Here is some of what they shared:

## THE FAITH TREE: GROWING, SURVIVING AND THRIVING GROWING

Money doesn't grow on trees, but faith does. Worry is interest paid on trouble before it is due, but Faith is like money in the bank.

Napoleon Hill wrote, "Faith is the starting point of all accumulation of riches." We often find we are where we choose to be. Faith gives us the courage to make necessary changes in our lives and allows us to grow in a clear and positive manner. Every dream shaped into a goal begins with the faith that if we plant a seed of hope, tend our garden with care and survive the storms that are sure to come our way, a thriving success will bloom.

When we began building our nonprofit, Childhelp, faith was the foundation; it became the soil in which we planted each advocacy center, residential treatment facility, hotline, adoption agency, foster care and group home. Soon we saw the fruits of our labor branching into national legislation and flowering into prevention education. We knew that advocating for abused children was part of God's plan and we would be guided through each season. We worked hard in the field every day but never doubted that a Higher Power was enriching our soil, nourishing our vision and ensuring the sun shone on our children.

But what if you have no faith? What if difficult times and disappointment leave you lacking the belief that you can be successful? The good news is that you can grow and know that you are growing. You can become stronger in faith, more knowledgeable in spirit and see it in yourself. A popular biblical parable posits that the smallest grain of faith, as miniscule as a mustard seed, can uproot trees and move mountains. Before you plant your tree, define successful growth and determine what will make your soil "rich."

When you choose to live your life in faith, desires and hopes will magnetize to you and you will begin to rise above the clouds. You will see beyond all seeming limitations and value yourself and others more. So ask yourself: Are you solely seeking monetary wealth or the richness of spirit that comes from being in the service of others?

## SURVIVING

After the devastating attacks on America on September 11, 2001, a scorched tree with broken branches was discovered in the rubble at Ground Zero. It was a small Callery pear tree that had managed to sprout a few leaves beneath the destruction. Its discovery rejuvenated the spirits of weary rescue workers and became a symbol of recovery. They were determined to keep the tree alive and worked with local parks & recreation professionals to plant it at the site where so much had been lost. Even when a terrible storm uprooted it, the tree was replanted and once again flowered with white blossoms of hope. It was named "The Survivor Tree."

Children who have been abused and neglected come to us with their spirits scorched and their lives uprooted. At each Childhelp Residential Treatment Village, there is a garden where the little boys and girls in our care nurture fruits and vegetables from seed to plate, learning the cycle of growth but embodying the importance of survival. We teach that there is no challenge of the past that can stop the fulfillment of a fruitful future. Like "The Survivor Tree", they learn that a small seed can create something great that may be uprooted time and time again but always has the chance to branch out and become whole.

What if your past is blocking your progress or you keep experiencing setbacks? There is no need to look back except to acknowledge the lessons you have learned, taking only the positive from these experiences to draw upon in your future. Sorrow looks back, worry looks around and faith looks up. Napoleon Hill asserts, "Faith is the only known antidote to failure" and 2 Corinthians 4:13-18 promises, "Though outwardly we are wasting away, yet inwardly we are being renewed day by day. Four our light and momentary troubles are achieving for us eternal glory that far outweighs them all. So we fix our eyes not on what is seen, but what is unseen. For what is seen is temporary, but what is unseen is eternal." When you release your struggle to a Higher Power, you not only survive, you plant roots that will keep you strong forever.

## THRIVING

Once you have grown in trust and survived the tests of your faith, you will enter a period of great power and responsibility. You will be victorious over your environment, weaknesses and all obstacles in your life when you follow God's path. This is your time to thrive! You have become confident in overcoming struggles and watched your dreams manifest. Suddenly, you can see the way in which a bright idea becomes a concrete reality. This is the final plateau of faith that Napoleon Hill so deftly defines, "Faith is the 'eternal elixir' which gives life, power, and action to the impulse of thought."

It is important to live and do your work in such a way that when others see you, their evaluation is the evidence of Faith. When that happens, you reap the rewards you rightfully deserve. One of the most important lessons we have learned is that success is not an endpoint and our thoughts shape each and every day. Our thoughts are our actions so positive thinking begets positive results. What's another word for positive thinking? Faith.

Matthew 12:33-37 speaks about using success responsibly, "The good person out of his good treasure brings forth good, and the evil person out of his evil treasure brings forth evil." The verse sums up perfectly, "Either make the tree good and its fruit good, or make the tree bad and its fruit bad, for the tree is known by its fruit." Thriving, then, is not just about how high you grow, it is ensuring that your branches never sprout poison bitter blossoms but rather that your fruit is always healthy and sweet.

Sara and Yvonne's Faith Tree certainly shows the depth of their giving natures, as well as their FAITH in each and every one of us. Let's review just a couple of their thoughts followed by how we can apply them to ourselves:

"Every dream shaped into a goal begins with the faith that if we plant a seed of hope, tend our garden with care and survive the storms that are sure to come our way, a thriving success will bloom."

*Your definiteness of purpose (goal) when nurtured with action and faith will overcome obstacles and create the success you deserve.*

"We worked hard in the field every day but never doubted that a Higher Power was enriching our soil, nourishing our vision and ensuring the sun shone on our children."

*Work hard every day but never doubt that a higher power is enriching your soil, nourishing your vision and ensuring that the sun will shine on your endeavors.*

If you are struggling to find ways to cultivate your own garden of faith, review the passage from Napoleon Hill and begin to harvest confidence in yourself.

## SELF-CONFIDENCE FORMULA

Resolve to throw off the influences of any unfortunate environment, and to build your own life to ORDER. Taking inventory of mental assets and liabilities, you will discover that your greatest weakness is lack of self-confidence. This handicap can be surmounted, and timidity translated into courage, through the aid of auto-suggestion. The application of this principle may be made through a simple arrangement of positive thought impulses stated in writing, memorized, and repeated, until they become a part of the working equipment of the subconscious faculty of your mind.

**First.** I know that I have the ability to achieve the object of my Definite Purpose in life; therefore, I DEMAND of myself persistent, continuous action toward its attainment, and I here and now promise to render such action.

**Second.** I realize the dominating thoughts of my mind will eventually reproduce themselves in outward, physical action, and gradually transform themselves into physical reality; therefore, I will concentrate my thoughts, for thirty minutes daily, upon the task of thinking of the person I intend to become, thereby creating in my mind a clear mental picture.

**Third.** I know through the principle of auto-suggestion, any desire that I persistently hold in my mind will eventually seek expression through some practical means of attaining the object back of it, therefore, I will devote ten minutes dialing to demanding of myself the development of SELF-CONFIDENCE.

**Fourth.** I have clearly written down a description of my DEFINITE CHIEF AIM in life, and I will never stop trying until I shall have developed sufficient self-confidence for its attainment.

**Fifth.** I fully realize that no wealth or position can long endure, unless built on truth and justice; therefore, I will engage in no transaction which does not benefit all whom it affects. I will succeed by attracting to myself the forces I wish to use, and the cooperation of other people. I will induce others to serve me, because of my willingness to serve others. I will eliminate hatred, envy, jealously, selfishness, and cynicism, by developing love for all humanity, because I know that a negative attitude towards others can never bring me success. I will cause others to believe in me, because I will believe in them, and in myself.

I will sign my name to this formula, commit it to memory, and repeat it aloud once a day, with full FAITH that it will gradually influence my THOUGHTS and ACTIONS so that I will become a self-reliant and successful person."

As I end this chapter on Faith, I want to share how I acknowledge and request support from a higher power. I have strong faith in God and believe in his abundant love. My faith was dramatically tested in December of 2012 when my youngest son died. We are not supposed to outlive our children. My life went into neutral, or into the land of numb, for several years. In fact, I almost retired because I was unable to find the joy in life. It was the people around me that challenged me, and yes, I believe my son even whispered in my ear, "Get over it Mom…you are still here for a reason. There is more for you to do." At the same time someone sent me the book, *The Prayer of Jabez* by Bruce Wilkinson.

The Prayer of Jabez is a simple 4 line prayer found in the Old Testament 1 Chronicles 4: 9-10 that reads:

***'Oh, that You would bless me indeed, and enlarge my territory, that Your hand would be with me, and that You would keep me from evil, that I may not cause pain.'***

This prayer has brought me great peace and faith. I say it every day and before every interview or speech so that I may add the greatest value each and every time. Below I share how each line impacts me each time I say it.

*Oh, that you would bless me indeed* – Dear God, thank you for blessing me with this opportunity.

*Enlarge my territory* – Allow me to reach a larger audience than I can imagine.

*Your hand would be with me* – Use me as your vessel and help me deliver the right message for the people before me.

*Keep me from evil, that I may not cause pain* – Help me make sure the message is a force for good and adding value.

In closing, I want to remind you that you are FABULOUS! No matter what you have been through, or what may have stopped you in your tracks…you are still here for a reason! And you can help others going through what you have survived. Have faith in yourself and use that faith to help others find the faith in themselves. And then ask yourself.

Have you added value to someone's life today?

I have faith in you!

~ **Sharon Lechter**

Author of *Think and Grow Rich for Women*, Co-author of *Exit Rich, Three Feet From Gold, Outwitting the Devil, Success and Something Greater, The 13 Steps to Riches, Rich Dad Poor Dad* and 14 other Rich Dad books.

# SHARON LECHTER

As an Entrepreneur, International Speaker, Bestselling Author, Mentor, Philanthropist, Licensed CPA for 35 years, and a Chartered Global Management Accountant, Sharon Lechter is the premier expert for financial literacy and entrepreneurial success. A lifelong education advocate, in 1989, Sharon joined forces with the inventor of the first electronic 'talking book' and helped him expand the electronic book industry to a multi-million dollar international market.

In 1997 Sharon co-authored the international bestseller *Rich Dad Poor Dad* and has released 14 other books in the Rich Dad series. Over 10 years as the co-founder and CEO, she built the empire into the world's leading personal finance brand.

In 2008, she was asked by the Napoleon Hill Foundation to help re-energize the powerful teachings of Napoleon Hill just as the international economy was faltering. Sharon has released four bestselling books in cooperation with the Foundation, including *Think and Grow Rich, Three Feet from Gold, Outwitting the Devil, Think and Grow Rich for Women,* and *Success and Something Greater..* She is also featured in the 2017 movie *Think and Grow Rich: The Legacy.* Her most recent books include *Exit Rich* in cooperation with INC Magazine and *How Money Works for Women with Wealthwave Media LLC..*

Sharon is a highly sought-after mentor and has worked with major brands like Disney and Time Warner and served two U.S. Presidents as an advisor on the topic of financial literacy. As CEO of Pay Your Family First, she has dedicated her entrepreneurial efforts to the creation and distribution of financial education books, games, curriculums, and other experiential learning projects. Everything about Sharon's career centers around impacting others to improve their financial IQ, access untapped potential personally and in business, and create their own legacy.

But everything changed in 2012 when Sharon's son unexpectedly died. All of Sharon's successes seemed to fade into the background. She kept working but on autopilot. She stopped playing at the level she always had and was living in neutral for a couple of years.

In 2014, Sharon decided to REFIRE instead of Retire and to play big again, and she wants you to as well with the Play Big Movement. It's time to shed the limitations that have stopped you in the past. It's time to play big, master your money and time and create maximum impact.

Sharon lives in Scottsdale, AZ, with her husband and business partner, Michael Lechter, a powerhouse in the area of Intellectual Property, Organizational Architecture, and Publishing. Together, they love spending time with each other and especially like to get away to their dude ranch, Cherry Creek Lodge (*www.cherrycreeklodge.com*), where they can get "off the grid" (literally) and get recharged for their next big play.

Sharon continues to be a committed philanthropist by giving back to world communities both as a benefactor and a volunteer and has been honored with numerous awards.

*www.SharonLechter.com*

*CHAPTER 3*

# POWERFUL BEYOND BELIEF

One of the most vital areas of our lives which we can control is our mind. Our mind is such a beautiful and powerful thing. It is powerful beyond belief. The philosophy of Auto Suggestion is truly the medium of influencing our subconscious mind, as Napoleon Hill explains as the third step to riches in *Think and Grow Rich* from 1937.

So, what exactly is Auto Suggestion? Auto Suggestion is the act of words that you say to yourself repetitively, with emotion and conviction, to seep into your subconscious mind. In other words, it's the process in which you are training your subconscious mind to act upon the actual thoughts you feed it. Keep in mind that your subconscious mind does not determine if the thoughts you are feeding it are positive or negative thoughts. It does not determine for you whether these thoughts are true or false, good or bad. Your subconscious mind simply acts upon what you feed it.

This, in and of itself, is either frightening to think about or really great news… depending on how you actually use Auto Suggestion and your subconscious mind. Most people do not

83

use the concept of Auto Suggestion and their success, or lack of it, suffers as a result. It's imperative to **YOUR** success to implement this concept right away in to your every day habits… or what I call "Habitudes."

Our dominant thoughts truly become our reality. What are your dominant thoughts? What are you allowing yourself to feed into your brain on a consistent basis? You know that saying, "You are what you think about!" It's so true. What you think about most of the day will create your pathway or Auto Suggestion to your subconscious. This is an awesome concept if you use it correctly and wisely. Let me share the 3 steps I follow to assure success in Auto Suggestion.

**Step 1:** Here is a simple exercise for you to practice daily and keep a record or a journal to log your results. Start to be aware of your thoughts. What I mean by this is for you to literally think about your thoughts. Start to realize and take notice of the thoughts you tend to harbor on and have linger in your mind. Grab a piece of paper and put at the top of one side the words: *Positive Thoughts*. On the top of the other side of this piece of paper write the words: *Negative Thoughts.* Now, start to log your thoughts throughout the day. Start to notice which you tend to lean towards. Are most of your thoughts negative ones, those of limiting belief in yourself? Or, conversely, are most of your thoughts positive and successful thoughts? This will take some training to gear most of your thoughts into the positive realm. But, don't give up. It simply takes practice. Napoleon Hill taught us that this concept of Auto Suggestion works for anyone and everyone. It does not matter where you came from or which side of the tracks you grew up on. He also teaches us to never give up, even if at first you fail. Keep practicing these techniques and you will soon succeed. It is inevitable.

**Step 2:** The second thing you must do is to start training yourself to only focus on the positive thoughts that come into your conscious mind. Do not allow the negative thoughts to fester or build. By allowing the negative thoughts to build up and consume your conscious mind, you tend to start seeping those thoughts into your subconscious mind in which you are negatively applying the Auto Suggestion concept. I use my Habitude Warrior technique I call the 'Power of 8.' It's super simple to use. All you have to do is agree to only give yourself 8 seconds to think about that negative thought that creeped into your mind—and then release it!

Vow to yourself that you will only allow positive thoughts to live within you. Giving yourself this permission is absolutely liberating. You deserve to live in a positive and abundant world. It's time you take back your own mindset and create the life you dream about.

Now is the time to start creating a list of affirmations that directly point to the ultimate outcome you are searching for. Let me be clear; this is not simply a list of random affirmations. This list of Auto Suggestion affirmations are geared towards building your subconscious mind to be open for success. They are essential to creating the neuron-pathways to connect your conscious mind to your subconscious mind. These affirmations will need to have emotion behind them.

They will need to mean something to you. The more emotion and conviction you have towards these affirmations, the better. Auto Suggestion only works with emotion and conviction!

Here is a list of some of my top 10 Auto Suggestion Affirmations:

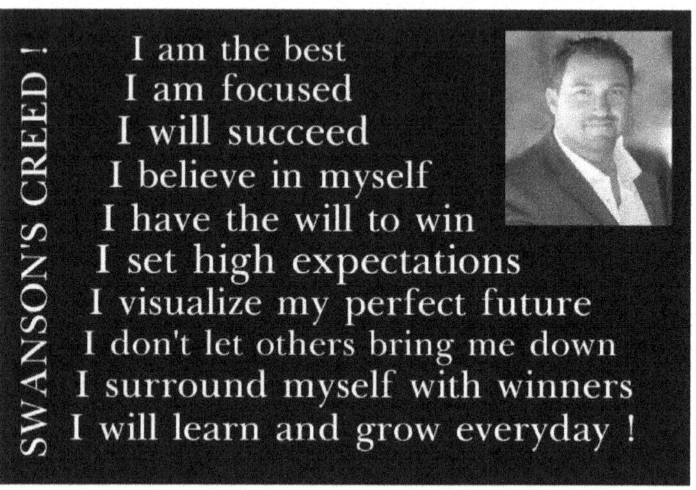


**Step 3:** Grab your affirmations and start repeating them to yourself throughout the day. Repeat them any chance you get. Actually say the words out loud so that you can hear yourself saying them. This is vitally important. You are now training your brain to accept these thoughts and affirmations into your subconscious mind. Don't stop with only your affirmations. Start to encourage yourself to seek out positive thoughts and use the same technique to enter those into your subconscious mind as well. Trust me, you will get really good at this. Make sure you write your affirmations and any other positive thoughts down on pieces of paper and leave them in places you

will find them throughout the day. Also, strategically leave them in places where you can see them before you go to sleep at night and also where you can find them as you get up each morning. Leave them sticking to your steering wheel of your car. Leave them at the office. Put them everywhere and once you find them, say the words out loud with emotion and conviction each and every time you see them.

Let's recap…

**Habitude Warrior's Auto Suggestion 3 Step Strategy:**

1) Log in a journal your daily positive and negative thought patterns

2) Create a list of positive affirmations directly pointing to your ultimate outcome

3) Constantly repeat these positive words to yourself with emotion and conviction

Mastering the art of Auto Suggestion will change your life! It's actually a lot of fun. I mean, think about it. How awesome is it to be able to master what you bring into your own mind? Too many people allow others to rent space in their mind and they aren't even charging rent for it. Don't allow others to determine your future and your outcome. Take control of it. In fact, take master control and point your life and success in any direction you desire. Our dominant thoughts truly become our reality!

# SELF-LEADERSHIP

## Napoleon Hill's Concept On "Auto Suggestion"

### Self-Leadership is:

*"How to Get Yourself to Do What Needs to be Done, When it Needs to be Done, Whether You Feel Like it Yet or Not."*

**It is how you mold the world around you and within you to assist toward your goal to live an abundant and rewarding life.**

In Chapter 4 of *Think and Grow Rich*, author Napoleon Hill calls this, "The Medium for Influencing the Subconscious Mind. The Third Step toward Riches."

This is about "ALL suggestions and all self-administered stimuli which reach one's mind through the five senses." This applies to what you permit as well as what you choose. The conscious mind is your gatekeeper for what enters your subconscious mind.

Hill recommends:

Read your written desire aloud twice daily and see and *feel* yourself already in possession of what you want.

Faith is the activator; you must *feel* the reward you seek.

Reading the words is useless unless you *feel* the reward.

You must mentally and emotionally *experience* the payoff you seek.

If you don't believe it consciously, then your subconscious won't believe it either.

Faith is the new skill you must learn to master.

We've all heard, "You've got to believe in yourself." Yes, that's nice to say, but how does one do it? The how—that is the master key to riches. Auto Suggestion is how you get there.

I've taught for decades that success must be M.A.D.E.

**M** - We need a clear Mental Image of what we want.

**A** - We need to live Affirmations of all types to reinforce our belief.

**D** - We need Daily Successes to give us real-world success experiences of all types.

**E** - We need Environmental Influences that grow our belief.

All of these are within your reach.

Wisdom and cleverness cannot shorten the path to success; they simply make parts of it more efficient. You must persist in this until the goal is reached. That's the price. No freebies are possible. Be exact and concentrate until you *feel* what you see. From this daily practice will come the Burning Desire that compels you toward your goal.

Assume the outcome is inevitable if you keep your "magnet" activated. Your magnet is the visual image and the resulting burning desire of what you want. Allow it to turn off and all the other forces of the universe will draw things toward them instead of toward you. Starting over may take you longer. Keep this practice in place daily.

Let the universe bring you what you seek. You must attract it through your mindset and actions. There is enough for everyone in the universe. There always was and always will be.

Your subconscious will reveal the practical plan to get your desire. Don't wait to have a plan, *experience* the payoff in your mind and heart daily now! Expect it!

When the plan arrives, act immediately! See yourself doing the work or service for which you will be paid. Close your eyes and practice this until it is compelling to you. Daily, daily, daily, daily— did I say daily?

**Become the person who will attract the future you desire.**

Acquire all the traits, habits, and characteristics that will make you the obvious go-to person for the opportunities you want.

J. Paul Getty once wrote a book titled *How to Be Rich*. Note the emphasis, not how to Get rich but rather how to Be rich. Many sad stories exist about poor people who won the lottery yet couldn't keep the riches. They had poor-person habits and thinking. They acquired millions of dollars with no effort and then they squandered it with bad choices. If you don't change your thinking, then any improvement in your circumstances will only be temporary.

## MENTAL IMAGE

I remember when I was a $525 a month clerk at the housing authority dreaming of future success. One day I fantasized about winning millions in the lottery. But rather than listing all the luxuries and indulgences I'd buy, I wrote out a plan for financially securing my entire lifetime and my family's as well.

On paper, I created a charitable foundation and a set of rules for selecting the family members who would serve on the board of trustees. The service was in a two-year rotation between members of my extended family so that everyone had a chance to participate but nobody could dominate. I made a set of rules that started with, "Any person who is caught lying or acting in a selfish or deceptive way related to this foundation will not only lose their position on the board, but they will be excluded from the benefits of this foundation forever and so will their immediate family members."

With advice from friends and people whom I admired, I crafted a set of rules for the foundation that would assure its survival long into the future and would allow every family member to benefit in meaningful ways from the money. No debt bailouts for spendthrifts, no special gifts for certain people, just financial security, and disaster-relief for all of us.

I never did win the lottery, nor did I create that foundation, but the thinking and preparation I did over those many months laid a foundation for my entire career. Yes, I did go on to earn millions of dollars and to achieve worldwide recognition in my field of motivation and human development. And for all these 40+ years, I've operated with a sound financial foundation.

The vision of what you want is your bedrock. That is what you create your Mental Image from. Then as you clarify the picture in your mind, the steps to make it a reality will come to you. Write them down and take action. Make it real in any way that you can.

Create a vision board or poster with images of what you want your life to be like. Make a folder in your phone of photos and images that give you the feelings you are seeking. Improve it constantly until it is perfect and review it often.

You cannot cheat your way to success. You can deceive others and gain temporary wins, but you'll become a crook. You won't respect yourself, nor will others. Bernie Madoff and other famous swindlers may have lived the high life for a while, but payment must always come.

# AFFIRMATIONS

Learn a new language, the language of success. Your words shape your mind, and your mind selects your actions. So watch your thoughts with care. Let me give you a few examples of how our words affirm either what we want or what we don't.

- When you say you can't, your mind hears it too. Our chosen words are interpreted by our subconscious mind as directions. It doesn't judge, it just follows and facilitates what it is fed.

If you MUST say "can't", then at least add "yet." Make your limitations temporary, not permanent.

- How do you talk about yourself? What labels have you adopted to describe yourself?

Do you say, "I'm the middle child," "I'm the runt of the litter," "I've never been good at math," "I just don't seem to be very (insert a category: creative, strong, sensitive, etc.," "I don't care about money or prestige, I just want a good life," "I've never been able to keep weight off," "I have big bones or slow metabolism," "You never know when things might go wrong." (Yes, you do.) "You can never be too careful." (Of course, you can!)

All of these are messages to your subconscious as to what to expect from yourself. Most are excuses for not living up to your potential. They are rationalizations that are designed to help you feel OK about being broke, left out, not proud of yourself, etc.

How about something as simple as "I can't remember"? How do you know you "can't"? When did you give up trying? Instead, say, "I don't remember yet." That's the truth, and it doesn't limit you from remembering. "I can't" means it cannot happen. "I don't" means that at present it hasn't happened yet.

- Refuse to criticize others. Don't buy into the soap-opera mentality that life is awful and then you die. Soap-opera TV shows feed on loneliness and fear. They cultivate the belief that nobody can be trusted, all will betray you, nobody is what they seem, and life is about greed, power, and sex. Stop it! Don't go there. Guard your mind and your language. Go toward the Light!

- Cold Calls – In selling, the action of making new calls on people you don't know is a critical element in success. Nobody succeeds by only calling on the people they already know unless they know thousands of them. And, if you wait for them to call you or to expect your call, you will have a lifelong wait. So, businesses encourage what is known as "cold calls."

Why cold? They say it is because the people don't expect to hear from you.

I challenge that. If they don't expect you, or you haven't called on them before, then why not use a term that describes the actual event? Call them what they are "New calls." Not "warm calls," that's just too juvenile. Besides, calls don't have a temperature. They are either new calls or subsequent calls.

So what? Well, if you make it a cold call in your mind then you will react accordingly. You'll feel unwelcome, like an intruder, and you'll be on the defensive from the start. You will be trying to justify the call. If it is simply a new call, then you can focus on your purpose: to find people you can help by selling your product or service.

- Here's another sales term that doesn't work: Closing.

"What?" you ask. "Surely you know that I must ask for the order if I'm to get the sale!"

True, but you don't have to close anything to do it.

"Close" means to shut, to end, terminate, discontinue, or finalize. We say, "the case is closed," this is a "closed market", she had a "closed mind", or "Sorry, we are closed. Come back tomorrow." All of these are acts that end or shut out something.

In sales, we want to earn a profit by helping our customer. That means we are forming a new business friendship, not a social one, but one based on mutual financial benefit.

You ask, "Do you mean that I should call it 'Opening' the sale?" No, of course not. But call it what it is: Confirming the purchase. You confirm a sale, you don't end it. A confirmation is the action that makes a purchase official.

Once the sale is confirmed, you begin a new relationship in which you provide benefits to the buyer and they provide payment to you. Nothing closed about it. In fact, you probably want it to lead to a lifetime of purchases and referrals.

Record yourself saying (with feeling!) what you want to become real. Say it like you mean it or don't say it at all. Treat this affirmation as you would treat an apology. Saying the words doesn't count unless the person hearing it believes that you mean it. Listen to yourself saying it, describing what it will be like, feeling the result.

Keep this in mind: whatever you say, you hear it too! Your mind accommodates what your words imply. "I hate selling. I just want to help people." That's the voice of fear speaking. That is self-doubt on display. The implication is that either selling is a bad thing, or you don't believe in your offer strongly enough to overcome reluctance to buy it. Can you truly help people? If what you offer is really worth considering, then why wouldn't you want people to consider it?

## DAILY SUCCESSES

When I was in the Army, I went through Basic Combat Training. Everything we did was part of a process to make us more effective in armed combat situations. We learned to obey orders from our leaders without hesitation and without challenge. We learned to jump out of bed at the sound of Reveille. We learned to march in formation so well that we acted as one body of men, not separate individuals. Everything counted because, in combat, our lives and other lives were at stake.

In Officers Candidate School, the same discipline was in place. How we made our beds, arranged our uniforms in the closet, shined our shoes, cleaned our weapons, saluted others all counted. Everything counted! We became highly aware of little details and very disciplined about doing what mattered, even the smallest things.

Daily life isn't military service for most of us, but the discipline and confidence that comes from achieving Minimum Daily Standards should be important to all of us. If you don't make your bed each morning, clean up after yourself, wash the dishes instead of leaving them in the sink, keep your personal grooming good and cleanliness excellent, then you will lose respect for yourself. Each small negligence on your part is like a word of discouragement from someone you respect.

Conversely, each small success helps build your confidence bank account and self-respect.

Find something in each key category of your life that you can achieve no matter what else happens that day. Feed your mind, exercise your reason, nurture your friendships, listen to your family members, exercise your body, observe your use of money, improve your work, practice your faith, explore great ideas, and have some fun! Whichever part of life you neglect will sooner or later interrupt the other parts to gain your attention. If you neglect fitness, then you will be forced to make time for illness, etc.

Do ONE thing in each area, no matter how small. If you want to become a runner, put on your running shoes every day and step outside. You don't have to run, but you must form the habit of showing up prepared to run. Once you master the micro-moves, discipline is within your reach.

Keep a record of every dollar you receive and spend. Keep it where you will see it. Become money-conscious and you'll begin to manage money better.

Spend 5 minutes in direct conversation with each immediate family member every day. Not incidental conversation but intentional listening and talking. Spend longer when you can.

Reach out to one friend every day and just ask how they are or tell them that you were thinking about them.

Contribute one better idea each day to your work. Share your improvements with others, but don't expect them to adopt them. Just share them.

Read one passage in the Bible or your faith text each day. Thank God for your blessings and list them each night when you go to bed.

Learn one thing today that you wouldn't have learned without trying.

Do a word puzzle or Sudoku math exercise or solve a problem today.

## ENVIRONMENTAL INFLUENCES

Look around you. What do you see? How does it make you feel? Encouraged or not?

Control what you can, adapt to what you cannot change.

You can structure your surroundings to be your helper. To clarify your Mental Image, go and sample what you dream of. Have lunch at a five-star hotel, test drive your dream car, take a snack and sit by the lake where you want to live. Rent a boat for the weekend or the day.

Go to the concert or club where you someday want to perform. Stand on the stage in the convention center or showroom where you will give a speech or receive an award. Buy a poster, or get a fold-out sales brochure, or a scale model of what you want. See yourself owning or using these each day.

Shop for the clothes you hope to afford, sit on the furniture you plan to buy someday. You don't need to go into debt, just get a feel for the items. Put yourself into the picture.

Get around people who share your enthusiasm and drastically reduce the time you spend around pessimists, doubters, and sourpusses. Don't participate in pity parties or criticism and bashing of others. Avoid political debates while you are seeking to succeed.

Choose the movies you watch with your goal as your filter. Don't go to occult or tragic or hateful or victim movies. Read uplifting novels, true stories, autobiographies, heroic, and inspiring works. Listen to positive podcasts, radio shows, webinars, and read blogs that lift you up. Manage your environment, don't let it manage you.

Create a vision board of images, a photo file, a playlist, slogans, tokens, symbols, and metaphors that make your goal more real. Start now to intentionally experience the success you dream about. Make it real, *feel* it.

Here is my personal story:

When I was in my twenties, I never expected to have a life that mattered much. My expectations were that I would get a middle-management office job at the phone company (where my Dad worked as a repairman) and retire at 65, then die whenever the statistics for my age group were up. I didn't have a college degree; nobody I knew had money and no one was encouraging me to achieve big things. My family loved me but didn't actively encourage reading, critical thinking, or aspiring to excellence or success.

One day, after hearing an inspiring message from Earl Nightingale on the radio, I started dreaming bigger. While working as an entry-level clerk in a government agency in Little Rock, Arkansas, I got a course catalog from the University of Arkansas at Little Rock and started listing the courses I would like to attend. There were more than 30 diverse courses that I found interesting, yet I still didn't know what I wanted as my career. I took a couple of night courses but didn't re-enroll.

Soon, I began to read motivational books and listen to recordings. There weren't many at the time, this was in 1972. I read *Think and Grow Rich* by Napoleon Hill, *The Power of Positive Thinking* by Norman Vincent Peale, and *How to Win Friends and Influence People* by Dale Carnegie. I listened to *The Strangest Secret* by Earl Nightingale and many recordings from Success Motivation Institute and Paul J. Meyer. Then it hit me! I want to do what these people do! I want to work in motivational training and be a speaker like Hill, Nightingale, Peale, and Carnegie.

But I had two limitations: I had never given a public speech and I had nothing worthwhile to say. That's a big limit! So, I started following the advice in each of their books. I set goals: lifetime goals, 5-year goals, 1-year goals, and daily actions to take. I wrote down my dreams and wishes. I clipped photos from magazines and pasted them where I would see them daily.

I changed my circle of friends by including people who also wanted to achieve great things and reduced the amount of time

I spent with people who were pessimistic or small-minded. I disciplined myself to use optimistic language and stopped running myself down. I began a discipline of doing at least one good thing in each area of my life daily. There were positive statements and goal descriptions on my bathroom mirror, the visor of my car, and in my notebook. Every day, I listened to motivational recordings… every day.

This continued for five years.

In the first three years of this life change, I went from being a clerk to being the staff assistant to the Board of Directors in the agency where I worked. I was elected president of our employee's association. I joined the Jaycees (Junior Chamber of Commerce) and became very actively involved in volunteer work. At the office, I got a raise, then a promotion and another raise.

One day, a man named Harold Gash came to me after a Jaycees meeting where he and I were both giving presentations. He said, "Jim, you have more potential than any young man I have ever known! You should come to work with me and sell Earl Nightingale's motivational recordings to businesses." I was aghast! Me? Sell? "But I'm not good at selling," I said.

Harold said, "Yes, Jim, you can be an excellent salesman. But first you need to change your thinking." He was right. I had the ability, just not the mindset I needed.

Over the ensuing months, I left the government job and worked full-time with Harold. As I listened to the recordings daily and made calls to tell others about them, I made sales. In fact, I did well and loved the work! Then the US Jaycees national headquarters called me and asked if I would apply for the job of Individual Development Senior Program Manager for the 356,000 members of the Jaycees.

On September 1, 1975, I went to work at the Jaycees HQ in Tulsa, Oklahoma. I was a full-time trainer and speaker in the field of human development, just like my dream goals had stated back in Little Rock in 1972. I flew all over the country and gave speeches to groups as large as one thousand. I wrote training manuals and collaborated with leading experts like Og Mandino and W. Clement Stone (Look them up). I met Cavett Robert, founder of the National Speakers Association. My life profoundly changed.

While at the Jaycees HQ, I still listened to recordings daily, read books voraciously, and had written goals on cards in my bathroom, desktop, closet, and sun visor. I was living a daily regimen of Minimum Daily Standards of behavior that would achieve my goals. I started jogging and working out, lost 52 pounds of fat and became an amateur athlete… at age 30. My life transformed!

In June of 1977, I left the Jaycees and went full-time into professional speaking. Since that time, I have delivered over 3,300 paid speeches to millions of people, done three round-the-world lecture tours, delivered a TEDx talk that has more than 2,400,000 views, authored 20 books, including three international bestsellers, served as president of the National Speakers Association, and received every major award given to professional speakers in the world!

Earl Nightingale called me in 1984 after reading an article I had published, and he subsequently published my audio program, coauthored with Dr. Tony Alessandra, titled "Relationship Strategies for dealing with the differences in people." It sold more than $3.5 million dollars' worth in the first two years on the market! Note: In 1972, I heard him on the radio. In 1974, I was selling his recordings. In 1984, he was selling mine!

Over the years since then, I have become friends with Norman Vincent Peale, Og Mandino, Zig Ziglar, Dr. Denis Waitley, Tom Hopkins, Mark Victor Hansen, Jack Canfield, Brian Tracy, Les Brown, Don Hutson, Cavett Robert, Patricia Fripp, Jeanne Robertson, and many of the great names in human development. I've worked with W. Clement Stone and done *The Fire Walk Experience* with Tony Robbins. I've had my own TV Show on The Success Training Network, hosted a daily radio show, published hundreds of video lessons with Clay Clark, and lectured in 23 major cities across China to hundreds of thousands of people. My books have been published in multiple languages all around the world and I've written college textbooks. I'm a professor for the School of Management at California Lutheran University. And... I could go on, but surely, you get the point. All of this was achieved without outside funding, a government assistance program, a diversity grant or exception to "level the playing field" for me.

I had no college degree, no money to start with, no connections with successful people, no mentor nor encourager to get me started. I was out of shape, overweight by 52 pounds, and had no skills that I could quickly apply to get started. My job was a $525 a month clerkship at a local office of the housing authority. What I have done isn't important except for the fact that: If I can do this, YOU can do this!

Your success will be M.A.D.E. by you.

You already choose which Mental Images to accept. Your words affirm your current state of mind and circumstances. You have daily experiences that reinforce the world you've occupied up to now. Around you are environmental influences at every turn.

**What I'm recommending is that you start making all of them INTENTIONAL.**

Take charge of the influences in your life that are having Auto Suggestion impact on you every day. Make your life what you want it to be!

# JIM CATHCART

Jim Cathcart, CSP, CPAE has achieved every professional speaker's dream: a Top 1% TEDx video, President of the National Speakers Association, Sales & Marketing Hall of Fame, Speakers Hall of Fame, The Golden Gavel Award, The Cavett Award, 21 published books, 3,300 paid speeches in all 50 states and 4 around-the-world lecture tours, and honored to be a Celebrity Featured Author in Erik "Mr. Awesome" Swanson's *The 13 Steps To Riches - Auto Suggestion* #1 Bestselling book series! He is a University Executive MBA professor, and he has also been happily married for 51 years, remained trim and fit despite prostate cancer and a pacemaker in his 60s. He plays guitar and sings in nightclubs and is a life member of the American Motorcyclist Association. Someone said he is what "Fonzie" (from the TV show Happy Days) would be if he had gone to business school. Starting with nothing but dreams and willingness to earn his way, he can clearly show others how to become the person who will attract the future you want.

*www.JimCathcart.com*

# CHAPTER 4

# YOU ARE SPECIAL

You may be asking yourself why I would say that, especially if I don't even know you. How could I possibly know that YOU are special when there are close to 8 billion people in the world? How could I say that you are special when I don't know if you have been struggling through the past few years, or have encountered huge setbacks recently? How could I say that if I didn't know that your successes have been really tough to accomplish and had taken much longer than you expected? You may be thinking that if I only 'knew you' that I would never in my wildest dreams come up with a saying such as: "You are special!"

Yet, I am here to tell you that indeed…YOU ARE SPECIAL!

This is such a vital concept to accept. It's vital to all of your successes in every area of your life. If you truly look at the possibilities that sit in front of you each and every day, you will be astonished.

Think about it. Just the mere fact of your existence is astonishing. I mean, it literally takes, on average, over 100 million little guys to swim upstream, if you know what I mean. Over 100 million of them, and yet just one is needed to create your existence. That is special!

Now, why would I mention all of that when we are discussing the concept of 'Specialized Knowledge?' Well, you see, the way I figure it is that we need to come to the realization that we truly are a gift to the world! The more you believe this, the easier it is to realize we must focus our energy and efforts into a special and certain "eld of knowledge to excel in such a magical way.

Too many people in the world simply go about their lives without harnessing their true magic or gift. They tend to stay in the general knowledge pool.

There are two types of knowledge, as Napoleon Hill describes. One is general knowledge, and the other is Specialized Knowledge. Hill mentions that people tend to believe the statement that 'knowledge is power,' yet it's not true. Knowledge is only 'potential power.'

It's time for you to vow to be an expert in your field. The beautiful part of this is that you can do this in a couple of different ways. The first way is to dive deep into absorbing as much knowledge in a specific subject as to be more advanced in that field than others around you. This will make you more desirable in business, for example, and organizations will seek you out as the expert in that field! The other way is to create what I call my 'Ambassador Team' or 'Dream Team.'

Your Ambassador Team or Dream Team is a group of individuals who are your 'Go To' team to educate you in those specific areas in which they are experts in. You draw from their expertise and apply their knowledge to the specific answer you are seeking. This requires that you are able to organize it and also possess the knowledge of how to put it all into action.

Your Dream Team is also referred to as a Master Mind Group. This is a group of individuals who all possess specialized knowledge in certain fields. It is very important to organize this group in such a way that all of the actual Specialized Knowledge in the group points to a specific, definite purpose.

I have a friend who is a very famous real estate investing coach who often tells me that he has over 7 or 8 Masters from highly sought-after universities. When people ask him how he accomplished that at such a young age, he replies that he personally doesn't hold any of those degrees. He hires his team under him in his company and has them on his payroll. So, it's as if he has 7 or 8 Masters underneath him.

There's a saying that explains you should never strive to be the smartest man in the room. It's smarter to surround yourself with others who are smarter than you so that you can draw from their Specialized Knowledge.

Once I realized the value of leveraging this strategy, I started to seek out how to create, develop, harvest, and sustain a successful Master Mind Group.

It took some time and trial and error. But, now I run a very successful Mastermind Group called the Habitude Warrior Mastermind (*www.HabitudeWarriorMastermind.com*), in which we have hundreds of members, all focusing on the growth of great habits and attitudes. We draw on each other's expertise or Specialized Knowledge to reach a common goal or definite purpose. Each of us contribute counsel from our own real-life experiences and expertise. Feel free to join us for a session and see if it resonates with you. Make sure you mention this particular book and chapter for you to receive one free session with us:

*www.HabitudeWarrior.com*

It's truly amazing to see the growth of each member. Wow, what a blessing to create these masterminds and attract such beautiful human beings who all have one major goal in mind—to assist and cheer on the growth of their fellow members!

Once I saw the true success of our Habitude Warrior Mastermind, I decided to create another group that focuses on the growth of professional speakers and authors. It's called the Global Speakers Mastermind. We bring in top Speakers and Mentors from around the world to share, teach, and inspire each of us in our growth as speakers, mentors, and Authors. If you are an aspiring speaker who knows the true value of consistently learning and sharpening the saw in your field, feel free to check it out:

*www.DecideTobeAwesome.com*

Another great friend of mine who is a highly paid and sought-after professional speaker colleague of mine has a fantastic strategy. He vowed to himself to read 3 books per month. The first book is on his specific field in order for him to consistently sharpen his saw in his own Specialized Knowledge. The second book that he reads each month is a book teaching him to become a better parent to his children on a consistent basis. And the third book he reads each month is on a subject that he doesn't have any prior knowledge of! It is so cool. He is constantly enhancing his Specialized Knowledge each month, and at the same time, he is learning new general knowledge that he can apply as well. Brilliant!

Mastering the strategy of Specialized Knowledge will forever change your life! It will truly bring up your worth and value in the world. You will soon realize that YOU are now the 'GO TO' person everyone else seeks out.

*MICHAEL E. GERBER*

# WELCOME TO A SPECIAL NEW WORLD

It has been thought by those at the heart of our business universe that general knowledge is essential for a business's success. Meaning, knowing how to do all of the essential things a company is both created to do and, in the course of growing in its market, forced to do, whether to compete successfully with all the others attempting to secure a foothold in that world each has designs to successfully inhabit, or whether, even more hopefully, to wrest a leadership role in that marketplace by overcoming all other competitors' efforts at same.

It's the general knowledge that begs this conversation, the belief that knowing how to do everything "generally" will forge a truly competitive enterprise into a market leader. Or, if not that, at least make one out to be competitive.

So it is that a summary review of all companies within any market, no matter what the product or service, no matter what its intention is, no matter how much experience may be put into play, that summary will reveal a surprising to most of us, realization that in the main, each and every one of those companies, look, act and feel very much the same.

Oh, yes, their name is different. Ford is Ford. Chevrolet is Chevrolet. And so forth and so on.

But despite the apparent differences between a Ford Mustang and a Chevrolet Corvette, when you walk into their dealerships, or watch their advertising, or talk to one of their salespeople, or go into their service centers, what you'll find will be, without question, very much the same.

Indeed, it's the un-bewildering sameness of the world of companies on our planet which is an almost eerie repository of the un-bewildering sameness of all our people, no matter their race, no matter their sex, no matter their politics, no matter their insistence that they're indelibly unique, one and all, as original as the day they were born. Uniquely, Sam, Uniquely Alex, Uniquely Jezebel, uniquely their own.

Oh, if that were only true! What we find, unfortunately, is exactly the opposite. Glaringly opposite.

The extreme ordinariness of our paths, of our choices, of our employment, of our work, of our creativity, of our discipline, of our hopes and intentions, flails out at even the most casual observer, especially when we're engaged in the pursuit of the special in the world of our so-called entrepreneurs.

I say so-called entrepreneurs, because that resides at the heart of the matter, the heart of the absence of Specialized Knowledge.

The heart of the dissolute fact that the reality of Specialized Knowledge is that in the broad universe of commercial activity here in America and, even more distastefully, throughout the rest of the world, Specialized Knowledge is looked upon, if it's looked upon at all, as a foreign, unnecessary, foolish idea wresting for too much time, too much capital, and far too much insistence upon creativity than is necessary to do business at all.

In this book, *The 13 Steps To Riches - Volume 4 Specialized Knowledge*, we deal with that subject in a most specialized manner. We look upon Specialized Knowledge through the lens of a universal creator. A universally inspired mindset that looks upon all things from the perspective of What, Why, Who and How? What are you there to do? Why are you there to do it? Who is responsible, and who is accountable for doing it? And How, pray tell, do you get it done?

In each and every case above, there is a special answer to those four questions, and a general answer to those four questions.

Answer them generally, and I will show you a company struggling to get by, if even that. Answer them specially, and I will show you a company in the process of transforming their marketplace and the people who live and work in it.

Allow me to demonstrate the difference:

In the general case, the What do you do might be said, to sell and distribute light fixtures to the residential marketplace in

Detroit. In the special case, the What do you do might be said, in the very same industry, to transform the state of light fixture distribution worldwide.

In the first case, we have an ordinary business doing ordinary work in an ordinary way. In the second case, we have an extraordinary business doing extraordinary work in an extraordinary way.

The first company has a strategic objective, exactly the same objective that every one of its competitors have within that very same marketplace.

The second company has a dream, an outsized objective through which to literally transform how light fixtures are designed, built, marketed and supported, worldwide. The first company is driven by a general description. The second company is driven by a special description.

To fulfill the first company's strategic objective, general knowledge implemented efficiently and effectively will earn it a competitively secure space in its local market.

To fulfill the second company's dream, Specialized Knowledge —Marketing Knowledge, Financial Knowledge, Enterprise Development Knowledge, Engineering Knowledge, Digital Knowledge, etc., etc., will earn it a leadership role in the worldwide community of the light fixture industry.

The difference between the two, is extreme!

The first calls for transactional skills. The second calls for transformational skills. The first is led by a transactional leader. The second is led by a transformational leader.

The way in which the people in each of those entities is inspired, led, taught, trained, managed, and developed are completely foreign to each other. Very much like a McDonald's store is remarkably different than a Starbucks store. Very much like the founder of McDonald's set out in his uniquely differentiated manner through which to design, build, launch and grow the only company of its kind in the world.

Just as did, however differently, the founder of Starbucks set out in his uniquely differentiated manner through which to design, build, launch and grow the only company of ITS kind in the world.

Astonishing, yes?

This is how we do it here, yes?

And in each of the above cases, it comes down to the very words a young women uses at the counter, to greet a new customers, to greet a returning customer, to respond to a concern any one customer might have about any one problem every single one of their customers has had, and might have, from the very first day in service, to the very day they're experiencing it, the minute by minute Special Operation of their Very Special company, doing their Very Special things they do, in their almost infinitely Special way of doing them, every single one of them, every single day, by every single employee, for one solitary, exclusively original purpose, to reinstate the McDonald's Brand, the Starbucks Brand, in the hearts and minds of those they were created to serve.

Which is after all what a Brand is, once said and done, isn't it? It's a Special Way of being in the world. And if it isn't, then what? Then failure, of course. Because that's why the vast majority of new businesses fail, 70% of all those started up in their very first year! 95% of which fail before they reach their 10th anniversary. Which then explains why Specialized Knowledge is not only important, but essential.

Because it is only Specialized Knowledge which distinguishes special companies and special people from everyone else. Welcome to the conversation. Welcome to a special new world. Welcome to a special new you!

Wishing you the most special of experiences as you visit the most special authors in this book series who follow in my footsteps in this journey.

**Michael E. Gerber** ~ Creator of The E-Myth.

# MICHAEL E. GERBER

Michael E. Gerber is the author of the N.Y. Times mega-bestseller, for two consecutive decades, *"The E-Myth Revisited"* and nine other worldwide bestselling E-Myth books concerning small business entrepreneurship, leadership, and management.

Additionally, Michael E. Gerber has written 19 industry-specific E-Myth Vertical books co-authored by industry experts, for Attorneys; Accountants; Optometrists; Chiropractors; Landscape Contractors; Financial Advisers; Architects; Real Estate Brokers; Insurance Agents; Dentists; Nutritionists; Bookkeepers; Veterinarians; Real Estate

Investors; Real Estate Agents; Chief Financial Officers; and soon to be, HVAC Contractors and Plumbers.

His mission is "to transform the state of small business worldwide™."

*www.MichaelEGerberCompanies.com*

*CHAPTER 5*

# IMAGINE THIS

> *"Man's only limitation, within reason, lies in his development and use of his imagination."*
> ~ **Napoleon Hill,** *Think and Grow Rich*

Imagination is the beautiful creation of a mental image in our minds so powerful and astonishing that it is believed to be real. It truly is what makes the world go around in my eyes. Without Imagination, the world simply would be stagnant and at a standstill.

Napoleon Hill teaches us that there are two types of Imagination - the Synthetic and the Creative. Although both are so vitally important to our success, I would like to focus on the Creative Imagination with you today.

In fact, I have created a new concept in which I use Imagination along with three other important components; when combined, literally transforms anyone's success quotient into a fantastic proven result!

127

# "VICI"

The concept is called "VICI," which implements four critical components: Visualization - Imagination - Creation - Implementation.

When I started working in the personal development world in my late twenties, I used to travel around the United States and Canada, training corporations and sales teams in various industries. It was a grueling job, to be honest. But it did give me the awesome opportunity to see the world, experience different cities and cultures, and meet so many individuals. It opened my eyes to so many lessons throughout those years.

One part of my job back then would be to conduct training workshops in front of strangers whom I had never met before and motivate them to take action on our company's offer for further training systems and seminars. So, if you think about it, I was a young guy in my twenties, just out of college, expected to go and train professionals who were older than me and most likely making twice the income I was at the time. To say that I was nervous at times would be an understatement.

I had to figure out a way to calm my nerves. I had to figure out a way to be the amazing and awesome individual I am and still get the fear out of the equation, at least pretend that the fear was not there. I had to do all of this without the strangers in front of me knowing what was truly going on in my mind while I stood in front of them. I was hoping they would not see the perspiration dripping from under my suit and tie.

I started to notice there was a direct correlation between my perspiration and my income. The more my fear showed to these strangers, the more my results and my income would take a dive. You know that saying, "Sweat and Tears?" Well, I started calling it my "Sweat and Fears!"

I really needed to change this around in my favor. If I didn't figure something out and quickly, I would have to reconsider what my career choice should truly be.

The fear was even creeping into my dreams the night before. If I knew I had an appointment with a team the next morning, that night before would be a rough ride in the brain of Erik Swanson while he slept.

Then one day, it hit me! I figured it out! I decided that if I was going to dream about these strangers every night before I met them the next morning in reality, then I would start to work on my dreams and win them over there!

Why not talk to them while I'm dreaming and get to know them there so that I would not be as nervous when I meet them the next day. I started to visualize them smiling and being very welcoming to me. I began to visualize them not judging me but actually enjoying my training and embracing my techniques. I started to visualize what types of objections they would have and actually visualize myself handling those objections perfectly in my dreams. This was such a game-changer!

Then I took it to the next level and imagined them applauding my speech and training. I imagined each one of these strangers signing up for our future trainings. I imagined that I already knew each of their names. I imagined they were great friends of mine already. Imagination worked in my favor in presenting to my mind something that felt like it was already in reality.

Once I had these two components all set in my dreams the night before each and every meeting, I took it to the next level. This would be the level of consciousness. It's also what I called the Level of Creation. In the morning, when I awoke, I would walk over to the mirror while brushing my teeth and start to Create the reality by repeating some amazing affirmations to myself about how this meeting will actually go.

I would say to myself things like: They love you! They respond to you in such a favorable way! They need you! They want you there with them!

I kept repeating great affirmations like this, and I would speak these words of affirmations out loud to myself. I would even thank them back out loud… even using common names. At first, it was hilarious. You could hear me saying my affirmations and then saying, "Thank you, John," "I appreciate that, Kathy," "You are so right, David!"

Once I had these three components down, it was time to suit up and conquer! Time for Implementation! I was so pumped up during my drive over to their offices that nothing could stop me — not even fear!

I would march right into their offices with a certain aura about me. People noticed that I was in such a great mood. People would start to smile at me for no reason. Everything just seemed to start flowing in such a positive way for me, no matter where I turned. Then, I started to notice that people wanted to surround themselves with this feeling and with ME!

Perfect! I'm ready! VICI was working! I started implementing all of the components while standing in front of these perfect strangers. And, wouldn't you know it, there would actually be a John, Kathy, and a David in the room somehow. Wow! Image that. I literally used the power of Imagination to create such a wonderful and beautiful environment. An environment in which I call your "PME," which stands for Positive Mental Environment. This is the environment in which we all strive to be in, yet many fail to achieve. You must subconsciously and consciously seek and create this environment.

Napoleon Hill was once asked if the art of Imagination can be learned as a skill. I am here to say it can. So, practice my VICI method and watch your results and your Imagination bring you to new successes in reality. In fact, let your Imagination go wild!

And for those who are looking for a sign (or a cool code), you may have just found it: "VICI"

# CHAPTER 6

# BE CRYSTAL CLEAR

Napoleon Hill taught us the value of crystallizing our desires into action in the sixth step to riches by the use of what's called "Organized Planning."

Organized Planning is what I like to refer to as the 'glue' that brings your desires into action form.Thisis such a vital step in the process of your success. If missed, you are literally throwing away the blueprint that brings your desires and goals to fruition.

It's simply not enough to set your goals and desires and wish upon them coming true. So many people around the world try that method which to you and I seems incredibly ridiculous. After millions of people read the book *The Secret* when it came out back in 2006, a fair amount of them tried to simply 'imagine' their success. Lo and behold, it didn't work. They were missing the extremely vital step of setting their blueprint or organized plan.

Can you imagine being hungry and wishing for a juicy triple-decker cheeseburger? You close your eyes and imagine it in your mind. You wait five more seconds just to make sure you imagined it correctly. You then open your eyes, and voila… NADA!

This is how most people set up their game plan for their success. Unfortunately, it is not a great game plan. Trust me!

So, what is a great game plan?

## SUCCESS LEAVES CLUES

One of the best lessons I learned early on in my career, while working directly with the amazing Brian Tracy, was the knowledge that success leaves clues. Brian would always remind me to seek out those individuals who were making a difference in the world, to seek out those super successful individuals who would either directly or indirectly mentor me. Why would I say directly or indirectly? Well, in this world, whether we like it or not, we are all mentors. We are all being watched by others. In fact, kids don't typically learn from parents with their parents' words. Instead, they learn from the actions their parents take.

So, if success truly does leave clues, then don't we owe it to ourselves to seek out successful individuals and follow in their footsteps by actually following in their footsteps?

I always love to remind myself and my coaching students that if you desire a certain, successful outcome, then seek out those who have tackled it before you and have succeeded. Seek out those people who are better than you in that particular area. For example, if I want to be a better chess player, I will learn and grow at a far more rapid pace by playing against people who are better than me in chess, rather than those whom I would normally dominate in the game. Such is the same in the game of life!

## WINNERS ARE ALL AROUND US

There is a fantastic quote by Napoleon Hill that goes like this: "A Quitter never Wins, and a Winner never Quits!" I love this quote because it's a constant reminder to always strive for your desired outcome. Those who never quit have such an advantage over those who have fantastic ideas, yet don't act upon them, or only act upon them if it's easy to succeed.

I have a great friend who holds the record for being in four winter Olympics over four decades. His sport of choice was the Luge. I asked him how he decided to pick that sport since he lived in hot and humid Houston, Texas. You don't really see too many winter sports being generated down in Texas! His answer &oored me. He explained that he had a burning desire to be an Olympian. Nothing was going to get in his way of this. He knew that he would never give up, no matter what. In high school, kids used to call him 'Bulldog' because of his tenacity and determination. So, all that was left for him to do was pick a sport. He started researching each sport that could lead him to the Olympics. He started to notice that the Luge seemed to have the highest percentage of athletes who were either disqualified, dropped out, or quit. He said to himself, "Perfect!" He figured that if he knew he never quit, all he had to do was 'stick it out' longer than anyone else, and he would become an Olympian! That's exactly what he did.

That story always reminds me of another story Napoleon Hill mentions in *Think and Grow Rich.* Remember the story about Thomas Edison failing over 10,000 times before he figured out a way to make the incandescent light bulb? Can you imagine if he quit? We would all be left in the dark. Yes, pun intended. The point I'm making should be clear: success truly does leave clues, and your job is never to quit.

## CREATE YOUR OWN AMBASSADOR'S LIST

It's now time for you to create a list of highly successful individuals to whom you look up to. I call this "My Ambassador List." It's a list of individuals who I learn from. These people have all been successful in areas in which I strive to achieve the same or better results.

Don't be afraid to reach out to these highly successful individuals. From my experience, the most successful individuals who walk our earth are also the most accessible. This is one of their Habitude Warrior traits. Highly successful people do not achieve the highest level without being able to connect with others in such a great fashion. This is to your advantage as it makes it much easier to connect with them. They tend to be very open to mentoring people in the footsteps they took.

## LEADERS AND FOLLOWERS

Once you have established the relationships with those highly successful mentors, it's time to create the blueprint for your organized plan. It is up to you to watch, notice, learn, and take action upon the strategies your mentors had taught you by their actions to their successes. Remember, success leaves clues, so follow the leader.

In life, we have two types of people. We have Leaders, and we have Followers. Also in life, we choose to become either a Leader or a Follower or both at certain levels in our lives. It's important to establish yourself first as a Follower to learn the secrets of success from those who have mastered that in which you strive to be great at. But, don't stay there. Make a conscious choice and resolution to become a Leader once you have mastered those lessons and steps outlined by your mentors, in which you followed. This is such a fantastic feeling once you have made that transition!

I remember when I made the transition in my speaking career. It's the story that I refer to as 'the time when Brian Tracy passed me the torch.' Wow! I was so excited for that day to arrive. I had been traveling for about seven years with Brian Tracy and the team, training groups around the world to become more successful in their businesses. Then, at the Javitz Center in New York City, in front of about 2,000 people in the crowd, Brian turns to me and waves me up to the stage, and hands me the microphone. This was one of the turning points in my life that assured me that I was moving into a leadership role in my career and in life.

It is your turn to transition into the new leader you were always destined to become. Lead the field and teach others by mentoring them to their success. Create your organized plan, stick with it and watch everyone soar around you, including YOU!

*MARIE DIAMOND*

# ORGANIZED PLANNING BY A TRANSFORMATIONAL LEADER

In this chapter, I wish to go deeper into how you can organize successful Transformational Leadership. I was inspired by the 10 major causes of failure in leadership and the 30 major causes of failure, both mentioned in the chapter Organized Planning in the book "*Think and Grow Rich*" by Napoleon Hill.

As a Master Teacher in the global phenomenon *The Secret*, which was partly based on the knowledge of the book *Think and Grow Rich*, I want to change the wording used in Organized Planning. Using words like failure keeps the subconscious mind focused on attracting more failure. What you focus on is what you get more of.

Transformational leadership is the leadership style of the 21st century. These leaders are inspiring positive changes in their teams and their clients. They are concerned and involved in the business process but also focus on helping their team, their clients, and the planet.

Some of the most Valuable Sources of Success with Transformational Leadership:

# HAVING A PURPOSE IN LIFE

Transformational Leaders have a personal purpose, a purpose for their business, and a purpose of contributing to Humanity. When you have nothing to aim for, you will not be able to manifest a difference in your life on this planet.

# ABILITY TO PUT YOUR VISION IN A DETAILED PLAN

Transformational leaders are able to take their vision and surround themself with a team to create a detailed business and marketing plan. While the leader holds the vision, (s)he is able to guide his/her team to bring together the detailed plan for the implementation and manifestation of the vision.

# BEING THE BEST

Transformational Leaders are not focused on small numbers or small results because they always have a large vision and focus on the big impact of their products and services. As they know when they are the best in who they are and what they do, they will reach higher and wider than others. It is not ambition that drives them but a cause of changing the world in a positive way.

# HEART OF SERVICE

Transformational Leaders bring forward products and services to make a difference to Humanity. Their heart is compassionate toward the planet and the suffering in Humanity. They will make a difference with ecological goods, planet-safe procedures, and create a diverse team around them, that supports each other. They are not asking this only from their team but use these values in every aspect of their leadership.

## GENDER EQUALITY REMUNERATION

Transformational leaders pay their teams for the combination of services, solution-driven creativity, and leadership. Salaries and remuneration are not influenced by gender, race, religion, sexuality, cultural background, and other dismissive inequalities.

## INCLUSIVITY IS PRIORITY

Transformational Leaders are aware of the talents and skills of their team. They ask them to use this to fulfill their own purpose and the purpose of the business that they have joined. There is no top-down business decision model, but a model of listening to the team before decisions aligned with the vision are made.

## INTUITION AND IMAGINATION

Transformational Leaders are in touch with their gut feeling or their intuitive side thru spiritual practices. They are able to visualize the vision with their imagination. They are surrounded by a team that is allowed to listen to their intuition and have the ability to think outside of the box with their imagination.

## GENEROSITY

Transformational Leaders are generous in honoring the work of their team with positive conversations, financial rewards, and promotions. They know that recognizing the strength of their team is more important than getting themselves all the honors and awards.

## POSITIVE ATTITUDE

Transformational leaders have a positive attitude toward their vision, goals, their team, and towards the future. They encourage others to have this positive attitude too. It helps the endurance and the vitality of the circle around them.

## LOYALTY

Transformational leaders are steadfast and focused on their vision and loyal to the team that supports them in building out their organization and manifesting their goals.

## ENCOURAGEMENT

Transformational leaders are leading by example and encourage their team to do so too. There is no space for fear-based communication but only for encouraging others to be the best in who they are. Their conduct, sympathy, understanding, and fairness are a demonstration of their leadership skills.

## OPEN COMMUNICATION

Transformational Leaders are not focused on titles, educational degrees, and backgrounds but only on the human potential of their team. They communicate openly with them with always the vision and goals as a guiding star.

## THE ETERNAL STUDENT

Transformational Leaders know that they never know enough about themselves, the world, and about leadership. They will always have a mentor, a teacher, a mastermind group, and books to guide them to learn more. Self-education never stops, and it is always with respect to the others. But it is more than education; it is applying as soon as you know the information so that your learning gives you results.

## MASTERING YOUR EMOTIONS AND YOUR MIND

Transformational Leaders do not lead by their ego. They have mastered their negative emotional reactions and thoughts or at least do not share them with their team. They reflect within before they have difficult conversations about team issues. Mastering Yourself is the key, or you will become the victim of your Ego.

## TAKING CARE OF YOUR WELL BEING

Transformational Leaders listen to their body as it is the vessel to manifest their vision with. Good sleep, an organic and healthy diet, regular exercise, daily walks in nature, meditation, and more contribute to your good health.

## KEEP MOVING FORWARD

Transformational Leaders know that there is never a time that is right; it is time right NOW. Take everyday steps forward, and the journey will bring you to Success. Do not allow procrastination to dominate your life. When the Universe has given you a vision, you have the responsibility to fulfill this vision to the best of your abilities.

## PERSISTENCE, EVEN WHEN THINGS ARE GETTING TOUGH

Transformational Leaders keep their eye on the finish line: manifesting their vision. Of course, there can be difficult times, hardship, lack of money, legal issues, and so much more obstacles. But they will persist as they know there is the Light at the end of the tunnel.

## WORKING AND LIVING IN A POSITIVE AND HARMONIOUS ENVIRONMENT

Transformational leaders know that you need to have a harmonious and decluttered space around you. As a Feng Shui

Master, I have been teaching this knowledge for more than 25 years. You can start this process by finding your Energy Number on my Free Marie Diamond App (Google play store and App store). Indicate your Gender and your birthday, and you will receive your Energy Number, four best compass direction, and video's how to start activating your office for Success and Abundance.

## PICTURE COMPASS

Your home is the unconscious expression of yourself. When I enter a home or office, I always look for signs to see if people feel powerful. As you are the Universe within, you need to be in power in your life. When you are not in power, you are not attracting what you really desire. Instead, you will stay connected with a poor consciousness and feel vulnerable and weak. You will feel that you are the victim of your reality instead of being the master of your life.

European kings and queens to the emperors of China and all political leaders had one thing in common: they sought a long and powerful government. They wanted to be the masters of their countries.

Your life is like a country. Your wish is to be the master of yourself and to make your dreams come true. What can you change to become the master in your Universe? Here are your first steps.

**STEP 1: Sit or sleep like a King or a Queen/ a President/ a Leader.**

Do you see the gifts of the Universe come to you, or do you sit with your back to them? At your home or workspace, you always need to see who enters, whether from your couch, dining table desk, or anything else you work on. Make sure you sit in such a way that you can see the incoming energy.

The Universe comes through the door and not through the windows. So facing a window and having your back towards the door is not efficient. The Universe walks in when you walk in. Even if you don't have any physical people walking in, you still come in, and you are the Universe.

You are not following the Principle of Power in the Universe when you come into your home and office and see:

In your living room, you are sitting with your back to the door, watching TV or talking to your family.

In your bedroom, when you wake up, you don't see the door immediately. In your office, you are sitting at a desk, but your back is facing the entrance of your office.

In a restaurant, your back is facing the entrance of the restaurant, or your back is facing the door when eating.

**Solutions**:

Rearrange your couches so you can see the door. Never have someone completely sitting with their back to the incoming flow of energy.

In your Bedroom: Place your bed on a wall so you can see your romantic partner coming in. When this is not possible, place a little mirror across the incoming door so you can see who is coming the moment you wake up.

In your Office/Workspace: Place your desk so you can see people walking in. When this is not possible, place a little mirror to the right or left and in front of you so that it shows you who is coming in from behind you.

Arrive first to your dinner appointment and make sure you can see the door and your guests arriving.

**STEP 2: Be Supported by the Universe All the Time.**

When you consider kings, queens, and emperors, you realize they are always looking to be supported by a Higher Energy and by their people.

A king or queen will always sit on a throne that supports their back and their neck. Their arms are resting on the chair. You wish to have the same support.

A true Master of Transformation allows support from the Universe at all times because, without this support, you are unable to fulfill your dreams and manifest your true potential.

Successful people always sit on impressive high-backed chairs. They are not sitting on small chairs without back support.

You are not following the Principle of Power in the Universe when you come into your home and office, and you see:
- You are sitting on a chair with a low back.
- You are sitting on a chair with slats.
- You are sitting on an old chair that is falling apart.
- You are sitting on the ground or on a pillow
- You are sitting on a couch without support for your back.
- You are sleeping in a bed without a headboard or on a mattress on the ground.
- You are sleeping in a bed with metal or wooden slats.

**Solutions:**

Buy a high-backed chair and place it behind your desk, especially when your back is facing the door.

Cover the back of your chair with fabric or place a pillow between you and the back of the chair.

Remove the old chair and purchase a new one.

Place a headboard at the end of your bed to support your head, or start by placing pillows between your head and the wall.

Place your mattress on another mattress, on bricks, or anything that brings it 30 cm or a foot from the ground.

Cover the metal and wooden slats with fabric or place pillows against the slats.

When you can't do anything like this, make sure you place support behind you symbolically: a religious, spiritual, or philosophical image or statue of support: a Saint or Angel in the Christian tradition, an image of the Letters of God, an image of a Rabbi from the Jewish tradition, the Koran from the Muslim tradition, Gurus from the Hindu tradition, Images of Gods or Goddesses, spiritual Teachers from other Eastern traditions, an image of the CEO or the president of your company, or just an image of a mountain (Not completely covered by snow).

Place a rock, a Buddha statue, an image of an angel, or any other image of support connected with your religious, spiritual, or philosophical beliefs behind your home, opposite the front door.

You can also place a large, round-leaved plant behind you for support.

## STEP 3: Surround Yourself with Power

The images/statues that are hanging around you represent you. The more powerful the images/statues that are in your home or office, the more you will be treated as a powerful person.

Depending on what you wish to accomplish and in what area you wish to be powerful, your images will be different.

When you wish to be a powerful scientist, then make sure you hang an image of Einstein or Newton in your living or working space.

When you wish to be an author, place books that have been read for hundreds of years; try Shakespeare.

Make sure you resonate with the images. If you don't like the person, don't hang it up.

### What are Powerful Images?

- Images of successful people in your profession.
- Images of award-winning people connected with your goal.
- Images of your idols and heroes, dead or alive.
- Images of famous people.
- Images of mountains.
- Images of your masters, CEO, or managers.
- Images of your certificates.
- Images of Buddha, Jesus, Angels, Saints, or Gurus.

- Statues of (fake) awards like an Oscar with your name on it.
- Front covers with your image on them (even if fake).
- Images of your products in a golden frame
- Images of royal or imperial figures
- Images of people you admire
- Images of your logos, ads, marketing material, articles
- Your vision board with your success goals

**Where to place your Powerful Images?**

Make sure you have powerful images at the entrance of your company

Place them in the North area of your office

You can hang them behind your chair to feel supported by powerful people

You can also hang them in front of where you sit to focus on these successful people

Place them in your personal success direction. Download the Free Marie Diamond App (for iPhone and smartphones available) and find out your personal energy number. You will immediately see with the Diamond Compass where your personal success direction is in the room you are standing in.

You can always place your Power affirmation in the north area of your living room, as it will impact all the people living in this home. Or you can place it in the north area of a conference room, and it will create power for the whole company.

**STEP 4: Activate your personal Success Direction**

You can also place more personal information about your Success and Abundance in your personal success direction. You can find your personal Success direction in the Free Marie Diamond App and with some videos to help you with implementation.

Marie Diamond, Master Teacher in The Secret and Global Renowned Feng Shui master with more than 1 million online students.

*www.Mariediamond.com*

**Extra tips:**

Make sure there is no clutter at the entrance or in the North area of your office.

Remove all images in your home that do not convey power or success.

# MARIE DIAMOND

Marie Diamond is one of the world's top transformational leaders, speakers, and internationally bestselling authors. A renowned voice on Law of Attraction, Feng Shui, and Dowsing, Marie Diamond is the creator of the Diamond Feng Shui, Diamond Dowsing, and Inner Diamond Meditation Programs. A 'seer' in a modern context, Marie was the only European star featured in the worldwide phenomenon *The Secret*. Latest movies she contributes to are *"Beyond The Secret"* and *"Thoughts become Things"* in 2020.

Marie merges her profound intuitive knowledge of Energy and the Law of Attraction, with her extensive studies of Quantum

Physics, Meditation, Feng Shui, and Dowsing to transform the success, financial situations, relationships, motivations, and inspirations of individuals, organizations, and corporations. Her clients include billionaires, A-list celebrities in film and music (Steven Spielberg, The Rolling Stones, Paula Abdul, etc.), top-selling writers, motivational speakers (Rhonda Byrne, Jack Canfield, Bob Proctor, Marianne Williamson, Vishen Lakhiani, etc.), world-class athletes, leading CEOs, Fortune 500 Companies (BP-Amoco, Exxon Mobil, etc.), MLM Companies (Lyoness, WorldVentures, Nikken, Herbalife,etc.). Globally, Marie has assisted government leaders, and governmental organizations in Belgium, Kazakhstan, Russia, Iceland, USA, Canada, and Mexico by providing comprehensive advice and solutions based on her expertise.

Marie is a Founding Member of the Global Transformational Leadership Council and is both Founder and President of the Association of Transformational Leaders of Europe. Marie has established a world-class reputation for transforming the success, health, relationships, and spiritual wisdom for millions of people. She is someone that thousands of entrepreneurs, businesses, and corporations turn to for unique insights and guidance with branding, marketing, and business decisions. She is also knighted to Dame Commander for her contribution to Humanity.

*www.MarieDiamond.com*

# CHAPTER 7

# DECIDE TO BE AWESOME

Napoleon Hill teaches us in *Think and Grow Rich* that Procrastination is the opposite of Decision.

I humbly have to disagree. Although Procrastination is a killer out there in so many areas of our lives, I believe the true opposite of Decision is Indecision—the act of NOT deciding one way or another.

You may wonder what the difference is between the two. I believe people procrastinate on so many things in their lives, yet they still have made the conscious choice of what they know is right to do. They have already decided what they 'should' do. They simply don't do it. For many reasons, people procrastinate because of fear, timing, ridicule, etc.

The act of Indecision is when people simply don't make a choice one way or another. Yes, it's true that by not making a choice, you are actually making a separate choice, which develops a series of questions into which you may be diving down a rabbit hole.

## DECIDE

One of the best habits, or what I call "Habitudes," you can practice in your everyday life is the habit of Decision. Literally, vow to yourself to make a conscious habit of determining which direction you will go in any area during your day. As we do the little things in our daily routines is how we do the big things in our lives.

Vowing to yourself to determine a Decision for each and every question that arises in your mind every day will assist you in training your mind to be laser-focused. This is a huge attribute people admire in society. In fact, this is one of our criteria character habits one needs to possess to be hired on to one of our companies with Habitude Warrior
International.

## ALL LEADERS ARE DECISION MAKERS

If you look through the history books, you will find that all leaders worldwide have been great Decision-makers. They simply use their inherent or learned habit of deciding to efficiently and effectively move to the next step in their process of that said project or mission.

Notice that I said they 'efficiently' and 'effectively' move to the next step. I did not use the term 'quickly.' In fact, true leaders use timing as a specific technique to decide and determine their correct outcome.

This is where 'Procrastination' may be misinterpreted.

## TIMING IS EVERYTHING

Timing truly is everything. You can have the best idea or invention, yet depending on your timing, you could succeed or fail in your endeavor. Think about it. If you only invested $1.00... only ONE.

U.S. dollar... in 1969, in something called Coca-Cola, well, you would never have money problems for the rest of your life. The rest of your children and grandchildren and great-grandchildren... You get the point. BUT, did you invest that $1 back then in 1969? It's simply not the same if you invest that same $1 now in Coca-Cola. See the difference? Timing plays a huge part in the action steps of our Decisions.

Making a Decision is great, but it needs to be followed by action steps. You could make Decisions all day long, but not followed by true and measured action steps in the fulfillment of that Decision, will only result in a 'desire' or 'wish.'

# DECISION-MAKING PROCESS

The secret to my Decision-Making process is pretty simple and straightforward. It comes from my love of the binary code. That's right, the binary code. Sounds sexy, right? Well, it's not supposed to be. It's a scientific and mathematical equation that we can rely on 100% of the time. It will never fail us. Our world, scratch that... our Universe, our Galaxy, our mere existence is made up of a series of 0's and 1's. That's it. That's the binary code. Let me explain my decision-making process without getting too deep into another rabbit hole, explaining binary to you.

## IF THIS, THEN THAT!

Based on the binary code premise, I use a technique that I call "If This, Then That!" Then, I simply ask myself a series of questions I call 'micro- questions.'

Our day consists of thousands, if not millions, of mini Decisions we need to make. These Decisions could be little tiny ones, and sometimes these Decisions add up to big, life-altering ones for us.

I take every one of these opportunities to ask myself a series of microquestions that question the actual result or outcome, depending on which Decision I make. For example, I ask myself, "If I do this, then what would be the result?" Or, "If I do that, what would be the alternative results?"

This series of micro-questions directs the conversation in my mind to force me to visualize and forecast my success in either direction, depending on the decision I make. Much like binary code, there are only 2 options, yes or no —each handing me a different result and outcome.

We have all heard the phrase: "The road less traveled." Well, it's true. What if the 'road less traveled' yields a more unconventional way of thinking and ultimately a better result and a better life? It's your choice. Choose wisely and decide to be AWESOME!

# SIGNIFICANT DECISIONS MAKE HISTORY

In *Think and Grow Rich*, the beloved Napoleon Hill states that Decision Making is the opposite of Procrastination. Most significantly, he documents through hundreds of interviews with the rich and famous that the strong, extremely successful, and wealthy people on the planet make decisions quickly and change them very slowly, while the weak, extremely average, and financially struggling make decisions slowly and change them quickly. Why?

In my experience, there are only four reasons why people choose to procrastinate and delay making decisions:

- Low sense of self-worth
- Refusal to live in the present
- Complacency
- Focus on the outcome instead of the process

**BUILDING AND STRENGTHENING SELF WORTH**

The implementation process required for you to become a consistent confident decision-maker begins and ends with an up-leveling of your sense of self-worth. The best example comes from the HVAC world of Heating and Air Conditioning.

In every home and office building, thermostats are installed that focus on inside conditions, measuring changes in circumstances that allow us to accurately predict and expect what the temperature will be. A thermostat is a component of an HVAC control system that senses the difference between the actual temperature and desired set-point temperature. The moment you set the thermostat, it triggers a furnace or air conditioner to run at full capacity until the desired warmer or cooler set-point temperature is reached. Then it shuts off the equipment until it's needed again.

In terms of our human set point, it is always dialed into the level of our self-esteem, sense of self-worth, and degree of personal development.

For example, how many times have we seen someone win 100 million dollars in the lottery only to be flat broke three years later? How many people do we know who go on a faddish diet and lose fifty pounds, but six months later, they have gained all the weight back and more. How often have we seen a wonderful woman do everything she knows how to do to get out of a physically and emotionally abusive relationship, only to jump back into a more devastating relationship with a bigger loser than the bum she just kicked out?

Why is this?

It is simply because of their personal thermostat. No matter what happens on the outside with money, weight, relationships, promotions of authority, ultimately, our thermostat is going to kick in to bring our outside world to match our internal set point. To accumulate more in the outside world, it is a critical unavoidable fact that we absolutely must become more on the inside. We must realize who we really are and who/what we have the potential and obligated opportunity to become.

## A FAVORITE ILLUSTRATION

When Louis XVI was forced from his throne and imprisoned, his young son, the prince, was kidnapped by those who overthrew the kingdom. They thought that in as much as the king's son was heir to the throne, if they could destroy him morally, he wouldn't realize the great and grand destiny that life had bestowed upon him.

Consequently, they took him to a community far away and exposed the boy to every filthy and vile thing that life could offer. They exposed him to foods that would quickly make him a slave to appetite, used vulgar language, and constantly exposed him to alcohol, dishonesty, and all things crude, lewd, and unrefined.

For six months, he was bombarded twenty-four hours a day by everything that could drag the soul of a man into wickedness and rebellion. But never once did the young prince buckle under pressure. Finally, his captors gave up on tempting and changing him and asked why he had not submitted himself to partaking of these worldly pleasures to satisfy his most lustful desires that were his for the taking.

With a deep and confident sense of self, the boy looked his captors square in the eyes and proudly proclaimed, "I cannot do what you ask, for I was born to be a king."

We all can become great decision makers when we stop procrastinating by focusing on the process instead of the outcome, refuse to be complacent, reset our personal thermostats and remember who we were born to be!

## LIVE IN THE PRESENT

The reason some people don't live in the present is because their present sucks! So, they medicate or live in the past, which causes pain, depression, regret, or a false sense of accomplishment. We all know someone who is stuck in the glory days, refusing to stop reminiscing when they threw that 40-yard touchdown pass in high school that won the game—"yep, like Uncle Rico, I was a superstar; give me more nachos and another beer! Burp!"

Why can't they see this and choose to let go and improve? It's because they continue to associate with those who force them to join them in their past. To be a consistent, positive, powerful, effective, and efficient decision maker, we must first stop procrastinating. This begins when you tell your procrastinating friends to stop dragging you into their past, reminding them that it's like robbing your old house and you don't live there anymore!

The flip side and other root cause of procrastination is to live in the future, believing that when 'this' occurs, I will be successful; when I do 'that,' I will finally be somebody. No. Living in the future creates worry, anxiety, and stress.

Napoleon Hill declared 'Thoughts Are Things' and the best anti-procrastination thoughts I know include: 'Today you have never been this old before—and today you'll never be this young again – so right now, and every right now matters. Which means no matter what your past has been, you have a spotless future. Which means you can't always control what happens, but you can always control what happens next!"

The practical application challenge to this truth is that if you sit around wondering if your glass is half empty or half full, you've missed the point. It's refillable! Thinking positively or negatively doesn't fill up the glass. The pouring does! It's easier to act your way into positive thinking than to think your way into positive action! Is this not decision-making 101?

## REFUSE TO BE COMPLACENT

As a teenager, I had been a Golden Gloves boxing champion, and Muhammad Ali had been my idol. I emulated everything he did, from tassels on my boots to the Ali Shuffle and taunting jab. With fast hands and a desire to beat everybody, I was known as the "Great White Hope." Each time I fought, instead of chanting, "Danny, Danny," my friends chanted, "Dali, Dali!" Muhammad Ali truly was my hero, and I would have given anything to meet him.

Years later, in 1988, I had just finished speaking to the students of Andrews University in Berrien Springs, Michigan. I was in the Union Building signing books when I overheard some students talking about seeing Muhammad Ali on campus.

I was so excited I could hardly ask where. They informed me that he was gone, but it was no big deal because he lived there and visited the school often. When I finished the book signing, I immediately excused myself and asked the two gentlemen who were driving me around to grab a camera and take me to Ali's home. They told me I was fooling myself if I thought I could meet him.

But at that moment, I decided to at least try. Leaving no regrets is always a powerful motivator. So is a sense of urgency: I will never get this chance again! They stopped at the big white wall and giant iron gate at the edge of a long, curving driveway. The gate was open, and the sign didn't say 'No Trespassing.' Instead, it said 'Welcome,' so I decided to get out and walk the hundred yards to his beautiful home. His eighty-eight acres had previously belonged to the Chicago gangster Al Capone, and "Muhammad Ali Farms," as Ali called it, was an amazing sight.

With my heart pounding, I took a deep breath and knocked on the front door. A woman answered. I knew from photographs that she was his lovely wife. She asked, "May I help you?" I said, "Yes, ma'am. Is Muhammad in?"

She asked, "May I tell him who is calling?" Sheepishly, I replied, "Yea, Dan Clark."

She walked away, and within seconds, an imposing six-foot-three-inch, 225-pound world champion, world peace ambassador, advocate of human rights, living legend, and idol filled the entire doorway. Muhammad simply smiled his famous smile and invited me in in his quiet, breathy voice. I excused myself for a minute, sprinted to the garden to where my friends could see me, and wildly waved my arms and whistled for them to come in.

In 1988, Muhammad's Parkinson's disease had not yet taken away his speech and mobility. For the next five hours, we sat in his living room and watched his greatest fights on his big screen, with his own personal commentary, jokes, and stories. He fed us and even performed his favorite magic tricks.

At the two-hour mark, I had realized that I needed to leave to catch my flight, but I made the decision to briefly excuse myself to reschedule my flight, so I could return to this once-in-a-lifetime experience! I'm so grateful that I did.

As we were leaving, Muhammad asked if I had any questions. I replied, "Yes. You are the three-time world heavyweight champion, which means you got beat twice. Over your career, you lost a total of five times, all to inferior opponents. Why?"

Muhammad's answer taught me the number one cause and only solution to eliminating complacency in our lives, "When you start looking at yourself as the competition and attempt to live off your past laurels and successes, you lose your competitive advantage and eventually lose the fight. Once the fight begins, you no longer hold the title but have put it up for grabs. You must do everything in your physical, mental, emotional, and spiritual power to win it back. Every time you climb in the ring, you must be brilliant at the basics, having outworked and out-prepared your opponent as a hungry, fiercely focused warrior willing and able to fight as hard as you did the first time you won the title - throwing every punch with power and purpose to do whatever it takes to win the title back!"

A paraphrased Theodore Roosevelt quote reminds us, "It is not the undecided critic or complacent who count. The credit belongs to the one who has made the decision to continually enter the arena, whose face is marred by dust and sweat and blood; who strives valiantly, errs, and comes short again and again, because there is no effort without error and shortcoming; who at best knows the triumph of high achievement, and who at the worst, if he fails, at least fails while daring greatly, so that his place shall never be with those cold and timid souls who neither know victory nor defeat."

## PROCESS VERSUS OUTCOME

Stay In Process – exchanging your focus on future outcomes for an extreme focus on the present action steps that will make the projected event and desired result probable.

Stop acting as if life is a rehearsal. Live this day as if it is your last. Whatever the present moment contains, accept it like you chose it, and work with it, not against it. Realize deeply that the present moment is really all you have. Excellence and greatness are achieved when you make Now the primary focus of your life!

Instead of fixating on the future outcomes – stay in the process and do those things at the moment that are necessary to achieve the projected outcome. Then, when you do, your desired results will come!

We saw this Decision-Making ability illuminated and in action on the same weekend during the National Football League Divisional Playoff Games, in which four playoff games came down to the very last play. Think about that. From an actuarial sense, the odds against that are immense to have every game come down to the final play.

Do you remember the game between the Buffalo Bills and the Kansas City Chiefs? A combined 25 points were scored in the game's last two minutes! Bills quarterback Josh Allen battled it out with Patrick Mahomes.

With 1:54 left to play in the game: The Bills take their first lead since the first quarter. DECIDING to go for it on a fourth down and 13 to go - Allen throws a touchdown pass.

Score: Bills 29 - Chiefs 26.

Buffalo's Center Mitch Morse said: "I wish you could have been in that fourth down huddle. It was just a lot of love. Guys saying they loved each other, 'Let's execute, let's do this for each other.'"

1:02 to go: Chiefs quarterback Mahomes DECIDES they need to march 75 yards down the field to score. In five plays that took only 52 seconds, Patrick finishes by DECIDING to throw a 64-yard touchdown pass to retake the lead. Score: Chiefs 33 - Bills 29.

0:13 to go: Allen DECIDES to drive his Bills 75 yards in 6 plays, throwing a touchdown pass to get within seconds of advancing to the AFC title game. Score: Bills 36 - Chiefs 33

With 13 seconds left on the clock, Mahomes DECIDES to drive his Chiefs 44 yards on 19 yards and a 25-yard pass. Kicker Harrison Butker (who had missed the previous kick) DECIDES to tie the score with a 49-yard field goal. Score: Bills 36 - Chiefs 36—the game goes into overtime.

Bills quarterback Allen never gets another chance as Mahomes & Co. DECIDE to drive 75 yards in 8 plays, with Patrick throwing an 8-yard touchdown pass to win the game and Divisional Championship! Final score: Chiefs 42 - Bills 36

After the game, Chiefs All-Pro receiver Tyreek Hill said: "Nobody panicked. Nobody was like, 'Oh, the game is over with 13 seconds left.' We just went out and DECIDED to make plays, and the rest is history. We have a great head coach, a great offensive coordinator, and obviously a great quarterback and playmakers. All of us made critical DECISIONS that allowed us to win!"

What's important in life is resilience. It's the ability to bounce back. It's the ability to have reverses. And then an inherent sense of optimism. Can you see the light at the end of the tunnel? If there's a barn filled with defecation and pony poop, can you imagine there's a pony in there somewhere?

The ability to be resilient and take the inevitable reverses that life throws at all of us is key. It's simple and nothing more than Decision Making 102 - preparing yourself so you can positively respond to rapid change!

At the end of the day, in every industry, every profession, and every personal and professional circumstance, you don't rise to the occasion under pressure. You fall to the level of your training. This means the pressure is not something that is naturally there. It's created when you question your own ability. When you know what you've been trained to do, there is never any pressure. That's why you continuously train, prepare and practice so hard!

## REMEDY

Seek counsel, not opinions. When it comes to making important decisions, let us never forget: some things are true whether you believe them or not; everybody is entitled to an opinion, but nobody is entitled to the wrong facts; you shouldn't believe everything that you think! Who do we trust in our world of fake news, with multiple contradicting opinions causing confusion and uncertainty? Is trust not at the heart and soul of decision making? Is trusting ourselves not at the heart and soul of making a decision?

Trusting ourselves begins when we acknowledge that every person born into this world was born with an inherent ability to discern good from evil and recognize right from wrong. We commonly call this ability our conscience, which means our conscience will never fail us. Only our desire to follow it decreases as we continue to do the wrong thing.

To illustrate, you and I were joined by a group of people. We entered a room that smelled so bad that our eyes teared up, and we collapsed into automatic gag reflex. But after only ten minutes in the room, it suddenly no longer smelled. Why? We had become desensitized, and the rank, smelly room was now the new normal. Is this not happening in our world of fake news where everybody with a phone has an opinion?

It's obvious that we become the average of the five people we associate with the most. So if you hang around five negative, whining, blaming, and complaining people, you will become the sixth. If you hang around with five obese, broke people who refuse to make responsible decisions about health, exercise, nutrition, and staying out of debt, you will become the sixth who can't decide to choose juice over soda and savings over credit card jail!

To become a great, confident, and consistent decision maker – especially courageous enough to make tough decisions that go against the status quo flow – the process is simple – not easy, but clear and doable when we get the facts, the whole complete truth, both the pros and cons. Study and learn everything we can about the subject or case in point. Counsel with unbiased experts. Ponder. And most importantly, stay true to your conscience by staying in tune with your natural intuition. It's called trusting your 'gut,' realizing that most of our significant and monumental decisions are usually our first choice, made quickly and intelligently by listening to our 'still small voice' of conscience, illuminated through intuitive promptings, made possible because of our strong 'thermostat' sense of self-worth, commitment to being present in every moment, refusal to be complacent, and focus on the process instead of the outcome.

# DAN CLARK

Dan Clark is the founder and CEO of an International Leadership Development Company; a High-Performance Business Coach; New York Times Bestselling Author of 35 books; a University Professor; a Primary Contributing Author to the *Chicken Soup for the Soul* series; International Podcaster; Gold Record Songwriter; and an Award-Winning Athlete who fought his way back from a paralyzing injury that cut short his football career.

Dan was inducted into the National Speakers Hall of Fame— and has been named one of the Top Ten Motivational Speakers In The World.

Dan has spoken to over 6 million people, in all 50 states, in 71 countries, on 6 continents, to more than 6,000 audiences, including most of the Fortune 500 companies, Super Bowl Champions, NASA, and our Combat Troops in Iraq, Afghanistan, Asia, and Africa.

Dan has appeared on over 500 television and radio shows, including *Oprah* and *Glenn Beck, PBS,* and *NPR,* and has been featured in the *Mayo Clinic Journal, Forbes, Inc., Success, Entrepreneur, Thought Masters,* and *Millionaire Magazines.*

Dan's extraordinary life includes soaring to the edge of space in a U2 Spy plane; flying fighter jets with the Air Force Thunderbirds; racing automobiles at Nürburgring and sailboats in Australia; serving on the Olympic Committee, and carrying the Olympic Torch in the Winter Games, and keynoting the United Nations World Congress.

Dan was named an Outstanding Young Man of America - and has since received the United States Presidential Medal presented by President Ronald Reagan; the United States Distinguished Service Medal presented by the U.S. Department of Defense; he was the national recipient of the prestigious Air Force American Spirit Award, and was named Utah Father of the Year!

*www.DanClark.com*

CHAPTER 8

# BE PERSISTENT IN YOUR PURSUIT FOR GREATNESS

In the world of success, persistence is one of the main key ingredients. Success in anything takes drive, passion, commitment, and, most of all… persistence! Without it, you will most likely quit your endeavors before reaching your desired outcome.

Luckily, persistence is a learned habit, or what I call a Habitude. It takes practice, but it can be developed and learned to assist you in anything you put your mind towards.

## PERSIST TO PERSIST

You can literally develop a new habit to learn the secrets to persistence. I will share the strategies I use to perfect this habit. But first, let's find out why persistence is so vitally important.

The reason why persistence is instrumental to our success is actually pretty simple. Studies tell us that humans are far more likely to "give up" or "quit" a task if we are not acting in a persistent nature. You know the law, "an object in motion tends to stay in motion." It is the same with humans. We tend to stay in motion once we start the action.

When I worked with Brian Tracy as a Senior Trainer and traveled the world assisting people in their personal and professional growth, we used to always be reminded by Brian that it takes far more energy and effort to start something back up once we put it down. He would instill in us that on the positive side, it's much easier to "keep going" on a task at hand as you have that energy and inertia helping you 'persist' through to your ultimate goal.

I've recently picked up the fine sport of biking. Wow, it's amazing! Yes, of course, I rode bikes as a kid growing up. And I continued to bike around everywhere I could throughout my life. But recently, I have really taken to it. I think it's because of all of the advancements in technology and the geometry that goes into all of the newer bicycles these days, especially to advancement and inventions of Electric Bikes… commonly known as E-Bikes.

So, just to be clear. I don't drink. No drugs. I do BUY BIKES! Yep, that's my passion and possibly an addiction now. But, hey, that's ok. It's a great addiction to have.

My point in bringing this fact up is that it reminds me of a movie that came out many years ago in the 70s. The movie was called *Breaking Away*. It was a great story of a young man from America who loved biking. All he could think about throughout each and every day was biking. He was so persistent in his thoughts about someday competing in famous races around the world and winning them all. He was persistent in getting on his bike every second he could find. If it was raining outside, he persisted and told himself to get out there and continue his training. He reminded himself that he had the mindset of a warrior. He reminded himself every day that he was doing what others were not doing. And, because of his persistent nature or habit he had developed, he figured other bikers would simply quit from burnout, which is exactly what happened. He started to notice that sometimes in life, you don't have to be the smartest or the fastest or the richest; you simply have to commit to your own persistence to not allow the possibility of slowing down on your own goals.

People will start to think you are crazy and sometimes even try to bring you down by telling you that you can't accomplish your dreams because they are far too far-fetched. Don't allow those negative thoughts to seep into your mind! In fact, stay away from anyone who tries to step on your dreams. I have a saying in my life that I follow every day… "Put in 'Mental Protein' rather than 'Mental Junk Food.'"

The young man in the movie was so persistent in his thought patterns to stay positive and keep on track that he ended up winning all of the races he entered. Was it tough? Absolutely. Was it worth it? Absolutely.

He kept persisting, and he ended up entering and winning one of the biggest bike races in the world—The Tour De France!

# THE PROCESS OF PERSISTENCE

1. Decide to be the type of person who will use persistence every day.

2. List and write down 10 benefits of persisting in the specific task.

3. List and write down 10 things that would be negative if you are not persistent in the task or you quit the task.

4. Remind yourself that you are a champion and deserve the accomplish this task and goal.

## MY PERSISTENT SUCCESS

Throughout my life, I have consistently hit each and every goal I set out in front of myself. My definition of success is when you reach and accomplish a worthwhile goal you have set out to achieve. The habit of persistence has helped me in doing just that. When life gets hard, and I sometimes feel like quitting certain things, I simply remind myself that I truly am a champion and a warrior. Then I read my four steps of The Process of Persistence. Sometimes, just a reminder is all you need.

*ALEC STERN*

# NO MEANS NOT NOW

Throughout my life, I have been persistent in my wants and desires. I found that if I balanced this with an action plan and didn't give up, I could reach almost any goal. I have worked hard and never had anything handed to me. At times challenges can weigh anyone down to the point of wanting to give up, but I learned how to overcome these feelings and keep my mindset and drive to win.

At 2 ½ years old, I was diagnosed with Perthes Disease, an issue with hip joint development and a lack of blood flow from the hips to the legs. This required a "no activity" lifestyle to let my hip bones grow and catch up. On average, it can take between 2-6 years to make this adjustment. When I was diagnosed, the treatment was simple: no walking, no running, and no physical activity, as this could aggravate my joint development and healing process. From 2 ½ to 5 ½ years old, I was confined to braces, crutches, and a wheelchair. My family traveled back and forth from Connecticut to Boston, where I spent about half of my young life at Children's Hospital for supervision and care.

Imagine not being allowed to walk or stand up at that age! While the diagnosis was very concerning, the aggressive "no activity" treatment had a very good probability of allowing my body to heal itself, and I could go on to live a normal life. As you can imagine, going through this was very difficult for my family and me. It really required me to develop the right mindset, desire, and determination at a very young age. There were times I felt defeated because I couldn't play like other kids, but with my desire to heal, I remained persistent. The doctors and my parents assured me that if I followed the regimen, I could overcome this. So I visualized myself running and playing like all the other kids. And, at 5 ½ years old, I outgrew my hip issue to go on and live a normal life.

On the lighter side, as I grew a bit older, on any given hot summer day, I would ask my mom for an ice cream. Her usual response was no. It would ruin my appetite; I would get a cramp swimming, I had ice cream yesterday, etc. My motto then, and to this day, is "no means, not now." As I visualized enjoying an ice cream cone, I went to work on the steps I needed to achieve this outcome. I would help my mom with a project she was working on or check off a few of my assigned chores. Then I would ask again, "mom can I have an ice cream?" Her response was, "dear, you have been so helpful today; yes, you can have an ice cream."

Today, in life and business, I use this mantra of "a no means not now." Often, when you receive a no, it can be the way in which you present what you are asking for. Perhaps it is an inopportune time for a myriad of reasons. Obviously, when you get a "no," it can be frustrating and feel like a failure. Sometimes we can be fearful of why we received a no, or we may want to blame others, thinking that they just didn't get it.

Instead, consider feedback a gift. If you ask for feedback as to why the person said no, they may share important insights with you. Or, they may prefer to not share any feedback with you. If you don't get the outcome you want from a conversation, ask if they would be open to sharing updates with you going forward. You can ask them their preferred frequency and method of communication for the updates you will provide. This allows you to cultivate the relationship and leave the door open. Over time, you can convert these no's into yes's. In many situations with potential customers, partners, investors, mentors, etc., with time and follow-up, I converted their initial "no" into a "yes," and we ended up partnering in business. This approach can also be used in life beyond business as well. In meeting and talking with others, if you set your intentions for a specific outcome and you visualize this outcome happening, you are setting yourself up for success.

Here's another example: as I finished college and started to seek out companies to potentially work for, I had an experience that took a definiteness of purpose, desire, and persistence to bring to fruition. Looking back, I am not sure I would have the chutzpah to do this today.

While in my senior year at the School of Management at Syracuse University, I was living in New Jersey. My mom was originally from Boston, and, as a young boy, we spent summer vacations and holiday breaks visiting relatives. I would often say I was going to move to Boston one day, and I visualized my doing so after graduating college.

In one of my college marketing classes, we did a case study on a hot computer company called Prime Computer that was based in Boston, Massachusetts. Prime was a new company and the first in a new space called minicomputers. Even though the company was new, they were well-funded and had filed for their Initial Public Offering (IPO). Mentioning Prime to my dad, his response was, "Who is that? You need to work for a large, established company like IBM!"

After learning about Prime Computer, I decided I wanted to work for them, so I set out to see how I could get hired by Prime. My first move was to cold call the corporate office in Boston. I asked to speak to the executive of Worldwide, Sales & Marketing. (Who in their right mind as a senior in college would cold call a senior executive at a major corporation to ask for a job? Me!) I called and was connected to his executive assistant. After stating my reason for the call was to talk about being hired for a job, I was told by his executive assistant that they were only hiring people with a minimum of 5 to 10 years of experience. She asked me where I lived. When I said New Jersey, she shared how Prime had a regional office in New Jersey, and I should contact them in a few years. I did not accept this response as I believed they would miss a big opportunity to hire recent college graduates. After many attempts and becoming friendly with his assistant, I finally got a 30-minute meet and greet. I visualized my meeting with the

Worldwide Sales & Marketing Executive for Prime and us shaking hands when he offered me a job.

The early morning of the day of my interview, I drove to Boston from New Jersey in a heavy rainstorm. I arrived 15 minutes before my appointment. I headed inside to check-in. Unbeknownst to me, my raincoat was shut outside of my car, dragging alongside my car door for the entire ride. Getting out of the car, I was met with the bottom of my raincoat covered in mud which splattered across my pant leg. I went inside and asked the receptionist (who laughed at my mess) to use the restroom. Stepping into action, I proceeded to wash my pants in the sink and attempted to dry my pants with the bathroom hand dryer. I ended up going to my interview in soaking-wet pants.

Luckily, everyone seemed to find this funny, so, despite my mishap, they were impressed and asked me to come back for another round of interviews. On my second drive up to Boston, I arrived 45 minutes early. I felt very confident, so I decided to look at apartments in the area. I stopped at an apartment complex and parked in the visitor parking lot to run in and grab some information. I left the car running as I thought I would only be a few minutes. When I came outside, I was surprised to find that I had locked myself out of the car while the car was running with my wallet sitting on the front seat of the car. I ran back inside and called a towing service. I begged them to come immediately. I now had only 25 minutes until my interview. The tow truck arrived and said that they couldn't open the car without a police officer present because I didn't have any identification. We waited for the police to arrive, leaving me only 10 minutes until my interview. The police officer said he couldn't allow the opening of the car without my providing my ID, which was locked in the car. After being very persistent, the policeman allowed the door to be opened, and I could show my ID. I then raced to the interview and pulled into the parking lot with 2 minutes to spare before my interview. My interview went well, and they asked me to come back. As an aside, my car was low on gas, and my leaving it running while waiting to get the door opened, I arrived at the Prime parking lot with only fumes of gas in the tank. After my interview, I had to walk to a gas station and purchase a filled gas can so I could drive the car to fill up for my return trip to New Jersey.

During the entire interview process, I had four visits to Prime over 2 months. Each visit for my interviews had challenges that I overcame one by one. On my last visit, we shook hands, and I was hired as the first-ever recent college graduate hired by Prime Computer! My desire and persistence had carried me through this process. No challenges or obstacles could get in my way or slow me down.

Initially, I was placed in the Prime training department to complete all the current trainings to see what resonated with me as a recent college graduate. I was tasked to help determine what was needed to build a curriculum for other recent college graduates to follow.

After 3 months in the training department, I was asked what city I wanted to be placed in for a sales/business development position, and my choice was Boston. I was assigned to a manager and team in the Boston office and was scheduled to start in two weeks. Arriving early, extremely excited and eager to start, my new boss called me into his office and asked me to close the door. With an angry tone, he said I was a liability to him and the team and that I had taken a requisition away from him that would have allowed him to hire a seasoned person with 5-10 years of experience. He went on to tell me "not to bother him or the other salespeople with questions." I was on my own. He said he would assign me some past customer accounts and territory and said, "Good luck."

At first, I felt deflated as it seemed I was set up for failure. I quickly changed my perspective and mindset and, instead, focused on how lucky I was. I set out to prove to all the executives who agreed to hire me that they made the right decision. Calling into the old customer accounts, there was resistance and, in a few cases, some laughter with comments like "why would we work with your company again?" So I started a dialogue with several company executive assistants and began to create a rapport with them. I then visualized meeting with these executives and shaking hands to do business together.

In one potential customer situation, I had been asking the executive assistant to set up a meeting with the decision-maker for a few months. When I would call, she would recognize my number and would respond with, "Hello, Alec. He still will not meet with you." I decided this time to press her for the reason he would not meet me. With persistence, I said, "I want to book a meeting, and all I ask is for 30 minutes of his time." She said, "You can't meet with him!" I said, "Why not?" She said, "Because he is out of the country for 2 weeks." I said, "Fine… I'll hold!" She asked to put me on hold. She then came back on the line and asked me, "Are you really going to hold on the line for 2 weeks?" I said, "Yes, I will hold." She put me back on hold again and then came back and said, "That was the funniest response I have ever heard. I will book a 30-minute meeting upon his return." She later shared she had a good laugh with the other executive assistants. After taking some ribbing from the executives, building a great rapport, and not letting up on my desire to do business with them, I ended up signing them as a customer and doing business together for several years.

At the completion of my first year in sales and business development, I was the overall company's "Rookie of the Year," outperforming all first-year new hires, including the new hires with 5-10 years of experience. I was also one of the "Top Sales Performers" overall, reaching more than 130% of my annual goal.

Given my success as the first, Prime went on to hire 80-100 recent college graduates annually, and I delivered the keynote speech at all the follow-on new hire training programs.

Through these challenges and many others, I've learned how to manifest outcomes by setting my intentions, creating a plan for the desired outcome, and visualizing the results I want. I don't let anything get in my way, either subconsciously through self-doubt or by external forces. For me personally, I lead with humor to keep things light and fun. By using this approach to pave a path to achieve your goals and desires, they can come true.

# ALEC STERN

**"America's Startup Success Expert"**

Alec Stern is an entrepreneur, speaker, mentor, and investor. He has become known as "America's Startup Success Expert" for performing hundreds of keynote speeches worldwide and for his popular sessions at top conferences.

He's been a co-founder or founding team member of 8 startups with 5 exits—2 IPOs and 3 acquisitions. As a primary member of Constant Contact's founding team, Alec was one of the original 3 who started the company in an attic. Alec was with the company for 18 years, from startup to IPO, to a $1.1 Billion-dollar acquisition.

Recently, Alec was selected to the Influence 100 Authority List by Influence Magazine and was recognized as The World Authority for Entrepreneurship by The Credible Source. In 2020, Alec was a 2-time Visionary Award and a Legend Award winner for his success as an entrepreneur and for his work helping startups and entrepreneurs. In 2021, Alec was a 2-time Award of Excellence – Keynote Speaker recipient at top conferences.

One of the Northeast's most accomplished entrepreneurs, he is a limited partner in Boston-based G20 Ventures, which provides early traction capital for East Coast enterprise tech startups. Alec is also an angel investor and mentor in a number of rising startups in various industries. Today Alec is innovating in a variety of industries like SaaS, Technology, Web 3.0, Metaverse, Crypto, Medical Devices, and Cannabis.

Alec is passionate about small business, entrepreneurship, and innovation. Working within the inner cities, or as he calls it, "urban innovation," is near and dear to his heart.

Only a sideman when it comes to music, Alec is an accomplished drummer and has had the honor of sitting in with a number of musicians, including Toby Keith's house band in Vegas.

*www.AlecSpeaks.com*

*CHAPTER 9*

# MASTER YOUR MIND IN A TRUE MASTERMIND

Let me just start out by saying that I had absolutely no idea what a mastermind really was. Even though I had read and studied Napoleon Hill's work for years upon years, I never grasped the true definition or reasoning behind masterminds until it landed right at my feet.

I had always thought it was one of those woo-woo kinds of mystical things people did. But, to my surprise, it's one of the most important and vital keys to my success and it can also be one of yours.

## GETTING STARTED

As I mentioned, the concept of masterminds literally fell into my lap one day. It was a number of years ago when I was conducting one of our Habitude Warrior Global Speakers Conferences. We had close to 1,000 people in attendance virtually at the summit that day. We had so many amazing, famous speakers throughout my summit.

One of the amazing speakers was my close and great friend, Don Green! Don is the President of the Napoleon Hill Foundation. What an amazing human he is! If you ever get a chance to meet him or even simply sit in a room with him, make sure you have your journal and a pen to take as many notes as you possibly can. He will change your life if you allow him to. I owe so much of my success to him. Thank you, Don!

Having Don Green at my summit created a magical moment when I interviewed him about the importance of Napoleon Hill's work. The subject of masterminds came up in the interview. It was super clear to me that our audience was very intrigued and interested in learning more about them. In fact, when we were diving into the Q&A portion of the interview, many of my guests and students raised their hands to ask more about masterminds. One guest even asked me if we provided masterminds to my students. I learned a great technique from my main mentor, Brian Tracy. He taught me to always answer the word 'yes' and then figure out how to provide it the solution. I did just that, and our Habitude Warrior Mastermind was born right then and there!

**SAY YES TO OTHERS BY SAYING YES TO YOURSELF**

This is such an important concept to learn and live by. By saying yes to yourself, you give yourself permission to learn and grow. You also give permission to others to learn and grow with you. If you think about it, had you not said yes to yourself in the first place, the magic of what you created would never have been born.

# GET PICKED FOR EVERY SPORT

Remember when you were growing up in grade school? I don't know about you, but I was never the most athletic kid in school. Because of this, I would never get picked first for any sport. In fact, I was only picked because there was no one left to pick. You may be wondering why I'm talking about sports right now. The reasoning is that since joining and creating masterminds, I have noticed that everyone is picked! A true, and amazing mastermind, if run correctly, will give everyone in the group equal attention. You will feel 'part of the in-crowd right from the start. We don't play favorites. We play equally and pour into each mastermind member to allow them to literally feel like they are family. They are.

Join a team who will be there for you through thick and thin. A true mastermind delivers results to everyone in the group. One of the organizer's goals is to make sure every member is 'up-leveling' to that next level of success. This is one of our visions and mottos in the Habitude Warrior Mastermind.

## SURROUND YOURSELF WITH WINNERS

When you join a mastermind, one of the most vital traits is that you are joining a team of winners. It is said that we are the culmination of the books we read and the people we surround ourselves with. By surrounding yourself, on a consistent basis, with the right people can serve to be one of the best things you can possibly do for your business, career, and personal life!

Allow your fellow mastermind members to become your cheerleader. In this day and age, we all need people to support us and cheer us on. Too often, we find ourselves listening and watching negative news and allowing that to seep into our consciousness and, even worse, our subconscious. It's time for you to take charge of your life. But don't do it alone! Another saying tells us that if we want to go fast, go alone. But, if you want to go far, go with a team. Find and go with your mastermind team!

## A TRUE MASTERMIND

So, what is an actual mastermind, and how can it help you? A true mastermind is a group that meets on a regular basis, either in person or virtually. Each meeting is run by an organizer. Each meeting's purpose is to assist each member, either directly or by what's called borrowed benefits, in growing in a certain and specific subject. Although masterminds differ, each meeting typically invites one to three members to sit in what's called the 'hot seat' or 'opportunity chair.' This is their opportunity to ask the group for their support and assistance in a certain subject or challenge they may be having. All members are responsible for giving counsel, rather than opinions, on what the hot seat member should tackle next to resolve the challenge. Each counsel should be based on the member's experience. The borrowed benefits are magically developed by all members taking advantage of learning the principles counseled on even though they were technically not in the opportunity chair. Win, Win, Win!

# MASTER YOUR MIND

One of the best gifts you can give yourself in this world is to master your mind. In other words, being clear in your life's purpose is vital to a beautiful experience as a human being. A great way to do this more quickly is to join a team of individuals with a common goal, direction, and purpose. Join a mastermind today! In fact, I would like to personally invite you to join my mastermind and allow your life to flourish as you have never seen it flourish before. Allow my team and me to introduce you to members who will become your allies to your success. Our members are cheerleaders waiting to assist you in your habits, attitudes, and business development. Don't go alone; go with a team who will support you in every step you make!

I invite you to meet all of us and check out our masterminds.

Please visit *www.SpeakerErikSwanson.com* to check out a list of our amazing and awesome masterminds! We look forward to meeting you and growing with you.

~ Erik "Mr. Awesome" Swanson

*BRIAN TRACY*

# THE POWER OF MASTERMINDS

Greetings! You have the opportunity now to dramatically increase your ability to earn and keep more money than you ever thought possible.

The richest and most influential people in America and probably the world have all discovered the incredible power of the "Mastermind." In interviewing wealthy people, they all recall that the turning point in their road to great success and achievement was when they formed one or more Masterminds.

Each rich person recalls the "turning point" in their life and fortunes. It was the same for all of them. It was when they started to cooperate and work with other successful people.

Many people struggled for years until that magical turning point when they met and began to share ideas with other successful people. Suddenly they were able to tap into the knowledge, experience, and skills of others. In almost no time, their ability to move ahead doubled or tripled – almost overnight.

The key to forming Masterminds is to look around yourself for one or more successful people and then determine how you can help them.

The key to tapping into the "Mastermind Principle" is to look for ways to "Give" before you get. The law of "sowing and reaping" says, "whatsoever ye sow, that also shall ye reap." This is a universal principle that works 100% of the time.

You have complete control over your future and your success without limit. But remember, the only part of this universal law you can control is the "putting in." The riches and rewards will come to you automatically, by "Law," not by chance.

From this day forward, look for ways to put in, to give of yourself. The riches and rewards will come to you faster and greater than you ever thought possible. Go for it!

# BRIAN TRACY

Brian Tracy is Chairman and CEO of Brian Tracy International, a company specializing in the training and development of individuals and organizations. Brian's goal is to help you achieve your personal and business goals faster and easier than you ever imagined.

Brian Tracy has consulted for more than 1,000 companies and addressed more than 5,000,000 people in 5,000 talks and seminars throughout the US, Canada and 70 other countries worldwide. As a Keynote speaker and seminar leader, he addresses more than 250,000 people each year.

He has studied, researched, written and spoken for 30 years in the fields of economics, history, business, philosophy and psychology. He is the top selling author of over 70 books that have been translated into dozens of languages.

He has written and produced more than 300 audio and video learning programs, including the worldwide, bestselling Psychology of Achievement, which has been translated into more than 28 languages.

He speaks to corporate and public audiences on the subjects of Personal and Professional Development, including the executives and staff of many of America's largest corporations. His exciting talks and seminars on Leadership, Selling, Self-Esteem, Goals, Strategy, Creativity and Success Psychology bring about immediate changes and long-term results. Brian Tracy is the recipient of many awards including The Habitude Warrior Lifetime Achievement Award.

He has traveled and worked in over 107 countries on six continents, and speaks four languages. Brian is happily married and has four children. He is active in community and national affairs, and is the President of three companies headquartered in Solana Beach, California.

*www.BrianTracy.com*

*CHAPTER 10*
# THE FOCUS HAT TRICK

*"The key to success is to focus our conscious mind on things we desire, not things we fear."*
*~ Brian Tracy*

Transmutation? What in the heck is that? Seriously, what is it? Okay, I think I figured it out! It took me years. But, I finally got it and can share it with you now. So many people get so confused on the term 'transmutation,' that I can understand the frustration and, more importantly, the lack of success in many people. Once you truly understand what the concept means and you follow its principle, true success is yours for the taking. In fact, you can also have a 'Hat Trick' of focus while using the principle of transmutation, as I did.

Let me explain…it's actually quite simple.

## WHAT IS TRANSMUTATION?

Transmutation has a metaphorical meaning to me, in which it refers to the process of transforming or changing something fundamentally. For example, transmutation can refer to the process of transforming negative thoughts into positive ones, or turning a difficult situation into an opportunity for growth.

So, transmutation is all about change. It's about taking something and transforming it into something else entirely. And let me tell you, that's pretty awesome!

In the world of science, transmutation refers to changing one element into another by altering its atomic structure. That's right, we're talking about nuclear reactions and chemical reactions. And that's some heavy-duty stuff, let me tell you. But it's also incredibly cool and awesome if you ask me.

But transmutation isn't just limited to science. Oh no! It can also refer to transforming something on a more personal level. Maybe it's changing your negative mindset into a positive one. Maybe it's turning a difficult situation into an opportunity for growth. Whatever it is, transmutation is about taking what you have and making it even better.

## TRANSMUTATION AND FOCUS

For many people around the world, it sometimes becomes a task to simply focus in on a specific area. For years upon years, psychologists have been studying the effects of 'focus' in people. They study and try to identify the best strategies humans use to have the best results when focusing on a single area.

My main mentor in my self-development life, Brian Tracy, used to personally train me how to use what he calls "single handling." Single handling is when you train your mind and commit to only focusing on one area for a certain time period. For example, you say to yourself you will commit the next 90 minutes to completing a certain task. You must commit and don't deviate from the task. Once you complete the task, you can set up a reward that you have completed it, such as going for a walk or grabbing a bite to eat.

I have done my own exhaustive studies in this area as well. What I have found is that when I use transmutation along with my single handling focus, I am immensely more successful in my ultimate outcome. Single handling focus is great, but implementing the transmutation concept into the equation yields much better results for long-term success.

## THE SPEED OF SUCCESS USING TRANSMUTATION

When consciously attended to, success in any area of your life is much easier to accomplish when attached to an ultimate outcome. It's even easier when not only attached to an ultimate outcome, but also giving meaning to the 'release' of certain areas that are not desired in your life anymore that does not serve a purpose. And, even easier and faster results are achieved when those areas you wish to delete out of your life are transmuted or changed into a positive area in which you desire to achieve and make into a habit for life.

# 3 MAJOR AREAS I TRANSMUTED OUT OF MY LIFE:

I make a conscious decision to transmute 3 areas of my life into 3 amazing success areas. It's one thing to consciously decide to delete something out of your life. But it's another amazing concept to use the principle of transmuting in which you change or replace an area with another positive area. Here are 3 areas that had a huge impact in my life.

1. **I QUIT DRINKING COFFEE!** I decided to take coffee off the table for myself. The reason behind this was simple. I kept finding myself reaching for a cup of coffee before I could do anything else in the mornings. This was becoming an issue. I found it funny that I made a habit of having to rely on something outside of my control. After seriously thinking about it, I decided to replace coffee with green iced tea so that it would be healthier for me and not give me as much caffeine. More importantly, I wanted to break the habit of having to rely on something each morning. I transmuted coffee into green iced tea and also decided that I would actually be 'coffee' for others in helping them be positive each and every morning; not only coffee for them, but espresso!

2. **I QUIT DRINKING ALCOHOL!** I decided to quit drinking alcohol altogether. This was literally one of the best decisions I have ever made in my life. I started to notice that I really wasn't myself after I had a drink or two. In fact, I started to notice my friends would start to ignore my phone calls when I tried reaching out to them. It wasn't until a good friend of mine, who was featured in the movie and book *The Secret* and

a celebrity author in our book series in *The 13 Steps to Riches,* John Assaraf, mentioned to me when we were out to dinner one night that he loves me, but doesn't love hanging around me when I've been drinking. He explained that I'm a great human, but a different human when I introduce alcohol into the situation. Right then and there, I decided I was done with that. I was done with something that didn't serve me at all. I decided to transmute my time and energy from drinking alcohol to writing books. Yes, like this book you are holding in your hands right now! Wow, what an amazing transmutation! I am now a 13-time #1 bestselling author and have created 5 separate #1 bestselling book series with over 120 clients as #1 bestselling authors in my series now. Wow!

3. **I QUIT NEGATIVITY!** I decided to make a conscious decision to get rid of negativity in my life. In exchange, I would transmute any negative thoughts into positive, awesome thoughts. This also changed my life! Our friend Deepak Chopra used to ask us if we were allowing other people to rent space in our minds with their negative thoughts. He explained that we were probably not even charging them rent for it either. Why allow negative thoughts into our minds? Why allow these negative thoughts to sit and fester inside of us like weeds in a garden? These thoughts or weeds will take over the whole landscape if we allow it to. I made a decision to transmute any negative thoughts into awesome thoughts and help others around me see that they, too, can change their mindset. This was the genesis of my motto which I call, "NDSO!" This stands for "No Drama, Serve Others!"

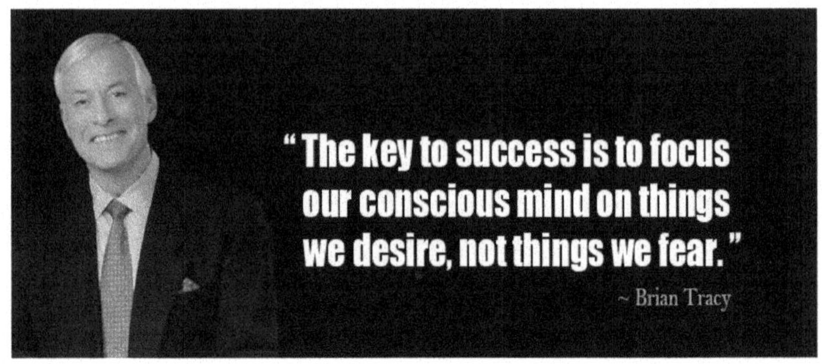


So, whether you're talking about changing elements or changing yourself, transmutation is all about transformation. And if you ask me, that's pretty darn awesome! So go out there and transmute! Make something awesome! Create your own "Focus Hat Trick" and see how your life will change for the better. You deserve it.

# GETTING TO "YES" ENERGY!

It is basic human nature to want to succeed in life, to dream of a better future, or just to surpass those who came before them. Nobody wants to settle, whether it's in education, the job you currently have, or where you are living.

Instead of working towards improving your life financially so that you are able to one day obtain your dream job, house, car, or lifestyle, there are too many people who would rather do nothing out of fear of failure or making a mistake.

Everyone has their own special and unique gift that makes them who they are.

Unfortunately, they are held back by their fear of how they are perceived, so they would prefer to deny their gifts altogether. In order for someone to use their gifts to their fullest potential, they need to be recognized, nurtured, and protected.

Transformation in someone occurs when they overcome these negative thoughts and transmute the energy to achieve their desires. Napoleon Hill described this as transmutation.

In my book, *Yes! Energy*, I write that, "One of the most vicious threats, deep at the core of people's failure to properly exploit their God-given gifts, is a toxic little offender called... *perfection*."

Perfect does not exist. There are no perfect people. There is no perfect world. While with the right energy and attitude, we can perceive everything to be perfect, trying to attain or achieve that state is a painful pursuit. Perfection is an ideal concept with no end in sight, preventing too many potential success stories from ever getting written.

Perfection does not allow for fast action or significant growth. Action is a gift. Using that gift means using energy to create, and that creation generates energy.

Part of the expense of doing business is the cost of wrong turns and mistakes. If a business or a person isn't willing to make mistakes and learn from those mistakes, there is no growth.

I try to preserve my energy by learning from the mistakes and imperfections of those who came before me. That's why I've had mentors and coaches since I was 17. I recommend always having a mentor or coach in your life. I believe in surrendering to a coach or teacher and letting that individual show me the way, instead of pursuing the route I think perfect for me.

Life lessons occur when learning from the mistakes and imperfections of those that came before us. You should always have a mentor or a coach in your life to help maneuver through life's obstacles. There are times when you will falter, the key is to get up, fix the problem, and learn from it. Those mistakes are there for you to learn from, so in the interim you will begin to make fewer and fewer mistakes.

In order to achieve the goals you want in life, you need to constantly change and grow. Perfectionists, however, do not like surrendering or making mistakes. Failing exposes their imperfection. In these cases, obstacles are avoided or denied, rather than confronted so they can learn from the experience and move on. Perfectionists do not pursue paths that contain obstacles, even though everything worthwhile has obstacles.

Too many live in this place of dreaming of success rather than taking a chance and seeing if it's possible. Worse, many do take a chance, fail, and crawl right back into the small place from which they came. You must fail a few times before you begin to succeed.

This stasis, this non-movement, is inaction. If action creates growth, then inaction shrinks a life.

Action is a gift. We are here to do and create. On the flip side, too many people get tangled up in a business that is not productive. People should physically embrace their imperfections. Instead, perfectionists strive to do every task as perfectly as possible but is the people who live their lives in abundance and fulfillment focus on their gifts of action and execution and cultivate an ability to perceive perfection even when everything is not quite perfect.

Our gifts are vulnerable to the attacks of outside and internal forces, which include, criticism, judgement, rejection, and indifference. The ability to take criticism well is a gift.

It is also a gift to offer criticism constructively.

If you are constructively criticized, you begin to learn what is helpful as you begin to live your life and what is not. If you are scolded in such a way that is traumatic, the lesson is less productive, and the gift of learning is damaged. This goes on throughout your lifetime, as we are always learning.

The ability to learn is one of our greatest skills, especially learning in a way that fuels our energy and builds an optimistic attitude by being able to take in good criticism and deflect the hurtful and mean criticism. In turn, we need to work on our capability to offer criticism to others that benefits them on a positive level.

Constructive criticism, given or received, should begin with an acknowledgment or a positive comment. I recommend the 5:1 ratio, or five positive comments for every one criticism. "Stay away from hurtful and get to helpful."

Putting yourself out there in the world sets you up for judgement. To combat hurtful remarks, you must use your gift of tolerance, for yourself and for others.

Think about the other person's perspective and try to understand if the judgment comes from an objective place.

Then you can decide how important it is for you to take on his or her judgment.

A big problem for many is that our affection for friends, partners, and family blinds us to their judgement. If you grew up in a codependent, dysfunctional family but don't even recognize that fact, then you're going to accept a lot of negative judgement that will deplete your energy and make you negative. Opening up your world to healthy people and enlightening experiences helps you find better sources of growth.

Getting rejected depletes your motivation to move forward. Getting rejected only means you move on and keep fighting. Getting rejected in either your personal or professional life feels like a personal attack. Hearing *no* is part of the process of getting to *Yes!* Make rejection part of the process of getting to where you want to be, but do not let rejection kill your gift.

Fortunately, you have the gift of fortitude. It feels bad to be rejected in one's personal or work life. All of it feels personal, but that feeling can be shifted with the right perspective. If you go out there and attempt to collect the *no's* in order to get to the *Yes!* then you make rejection part of the process.

Some might say that indifference is the cruelest attack on one's gifts. While criticism, judgment, and rejection are hurtful, they are at least active, if not negative, acknowledgments of one's gifts.

Indifference, though, is not reality for those who live in extreme energy. It only means that your gifts are being displayed in the wrong arena. The gifts of faith and certainty help us stay optimistic and energized.

When we truly recognize our gifts, we realize that these are not skills we created, but rather talents we were given and with which we were entrusted. If you truly believe in your mission and motives and are celebrating your gifts by using them, then no amount of indifference can get in your way.

If you drop your burdens, you can change the conversation to a new story. This progress, and that progress may lead to success. Plans rarely go exactly as you think they will, and success may not look the way you thought it would, but forward motion always puts you a step ahead of where you were and want to be.

Fear, guilt, shame, embarrassment, and small thinking are all adversaries that can attack our gifts and cause severe damage.

Fear being the biggest saboteur out there preys on what we are afraid of, which includes failure, rejection, trying something new, or our fear of wasted effort or potential disappointment.

Are you really afraid of failing or are you afraid of succeeding and the enormous responsibility of success that comes with it? Even if you don't succeed, or at least don't succeed in the way you wanted, you still did something. That experience of making an effort will make the next effort that much easier.

Moving forward always puts you a step ahead of where you were, even though plans rarely go exactly as you think they will, and success may not look the way you thought it would.

Many people quit when they come upon those last few troubling obstacles. If you are fully exploiting your gifts, doing all you are capable of, and blasting into extreme energy, you can stay on track.

We feel selfish or unjustified in recognizing our gifts, so we play small. You cannot help anyone else until you have helped yourself, and if you're constrained or struggling in any way, then you don't have the freedom and energy to help others. By acknowledging your gifts, you empower yourself to create abundance for yourself and those you love.

As I've mentioned before, playing small is bad for you and those around you; it serves nothing and no one. When people engage scarcity thinking and believe that there is not enough, they fight and compete, and create fear and anxiety. If only you understood that there is more than enough for everyone, you would go get it with abandon.

Opportunity is about finding the right thing at the right time, not about numbers.

Confidence is a gift and truly believing in yourself and your gifts, can overcome guilt, shame, and embarrassment. Trust yourself and your abilities. This will inspire and uplift others to do the same.

Negative criticism and harsh judgment conditions you to thinking small while playing to lose. As with external criticism and judgment, our internal criticism and judgment can attack our gifts and be a detriment to our energy and optimism. These internal messages allow us to think that we are not good enough. Not good enough to accomplish more than the average person, not good enough to stand out from the crowd, not good enough to lead, an not even good enough to have a life that goes beyond basic survival.

There are many models of what abundance and excellence look like out there, and you can learn from, and become, one of them. Even these lives don't exemplify perfection, because there is no such thing. Life can be great without being perfect.

You can lead a life as fabulous as the one you perceive someone else is having without being perfect. The gift of unlimited human potential is yours as much as it is anyone else's.

If we as humans did not progress and grow, we would risk getting smaller and possibly evolving backward to a place of less ease and comfort, and more fear and despair. The gift of unlimited human potential must be nourished in order to attack small thinking. It begins with changing the conversation. Ask "Why?" Don't let something be just because it has always been that way. Too many people seek permission and follow others. Living your gifts is exploiting your gifts.

When you get a progressive, exciting, energizing idea in your head, consider how that new thought got delivered into your head in the first place. Those thoughts and ideas may be gifts. It's your duty to celebrate and exploit them.

We can have abundant, fun lives that are lived responsibly. That concept is the new conversation, and it begins by shifting our view of our place in this world.

Education cannot be passive. Children shouldn't receive anything, they should dig in actively and take their education.

Let's up the education ante by changing the system, helping children think creatively and expansively, tapping into all their skills, using even their latent and unique gifts.

There is too much focus on jobs, and the expectation that most people in this world is that they will go out and get a job, because they have to have one and that they deserve one.

Jobs do not encourage people to use their God-given talents and gifts. The United States was built on the entrepreneurial spirit to create.

Thanks to our freedom, our rights, and our liberties, no one has to buy into the economy and community into which they are born. Throughout history, people have created their own microeconomics where they find their talents and gifts, and then they have traded and leveraged those skills, as well as their resources.

Interdependent entrepreneurs is a party into which anyone can invite themselves. It requires recognizing that everything is not perfect. It requires seeing a demand and creating a supply, filling a niche or void, or empowering a chain by providing a stronger link.

This perspective of the economy and community changes the conversation and allows individuals to use their gifts.

Working hard and making a lot of money is an unreal correlation. There are plenty of people who have worked hard and gotten nowhere. On the other hand, there are those who have substantial wealth and didn't break a sweat. Those who know their gifts and use their strengths do not have to work as hard as those who depend on others and do the work they are told rather than the work at which they excel.

Planning to retire is planning to die. Retirement cannot be the endgame. i switch out the term retirement for Freedom Day –a time in your life when you can do what you want, when and with whom you want. Because you can.

There are so many areas in which we fail to live up to our gifts because we are afraid of being less than perfect.

If you are going to try to do a lot in this life, you are going to be wrong sometimes. In order to even attempt to change the conversation, you are going to have to allow yourself to try out new ideas and thoughts. Opening up a dialogue only to rationalize, defend, or justify closes down the avenues of growth.

Face it, when working to achieve your goals, you are going to look stupid sometimes. When you collect experiences that create the evidence you need in order to be confident, you are going to look stupid. Being vulnerable to saying and doing stupid things helps you strengthen your gifts. It builds your lightness, your humility, and your candor, and your empathy. The best gift, in these cases, is your sense of humor.

Life can be so much bigger and better if you are willing to let go of "perfect." Allow perfect to be perception, not reality, and every day of your life will be a happy one. Let go of perfect and you will let in a lot more excitement, energy, and optimism than you ever thought possible. This will attract others, and soon you will be part of a whole new team.

# LORAL LANGEMEIER

Loral Langemeier is a money expert, sought-after speaker, entrepreneurial thought leader, and bestselling author of five books. Her goal is to change the conversation people have about money worldwide and empower people to become millionaires.

The CEO and Founder of Live Out Loud, Inc. – a multinational organization—Loral relentlessly and candidly shares her best advice without hesitation or apology. What sets her apart from other wealth experts is her innate ability to recognize and acknowledge the skills & talents of people, inspiring them to generate wealth.

She has created, nurtured, and perfected a 3-5 year strategy to make millions for the "Average Jill and Joe." To date, she and her team have served thousands of individuals worldwide and created hundreds of millionaires through wealth-building education keynotes, workshops, products, events, programs, and coaching services.

Loral is living proof that it makes no difference where you start in life; anyone can have the life of his or her dreams. Loral is a money expert, bestselling author, and Owner & CEO of Integrated Wealth Systems—A wealth coaching company.

Growing up on her family's farm in Nebraska, Loral learned the value of hard work, persistence and how to get things done even in the face of much opposition and criticism.

Loral began her career working for the Chevron Corporation right out of college. It was clear to her early on that there was more to life than cubicles and trading her time for dollars. Despite her own fears and persuasion from friends and family against it, Loral quit her job at Chevron to become an Executive Coach.

Virtually overnight, Loral quintupled her income as an Executive Coach, while working much less. With her newfound freedom of time and accumulation of wealth she founded Live Out Loud, Inc. As a single mother, Loral has since dedicated her life to helping men and women from all walks of life to become millionaires and have time to spend with their families.

Loral's straight talk and charming personality electrifies audiences and inspires powerful action from live stages and television programs ranging from CNN, CNBC, The Street TV, Fox News Channel, Fox Business Channel-America's Nightly Scoreboard, The Dr. Phil Show, and The View. She is a regular guest-host on The Circle in Australia and has been featured in articles in USA Today, The Wall Street Journal, The New York Times, Forbes Magazine and was the breakout star in the film The Secret.

*www.LoralLangemeier.com*

# CHAPTER 11

# CONGRUENCY IS THE KEY FACTOR

*"Act with purpose, courage, confidence, competence and intelligence until these qualities 'lock in' to your subconscious mind."*
~ Brian Tracy

What is the real difference between the conscious mind and the subconscious mind? The conscious mind and the subconscious mind are two distinct aspects of our mental processes.

The conscious mind refers to our awareness of our thoughts, feelings, sensations, and perceptions in the present moment. It is responsible for our logical thinking, decision-making, and our ability to process information consciously. When we are consciously aware of something, we can actively focus our attention on it and direct our thoughts and actions accordingly.

On the other hand, the subconscious mind, also known as the unconscious mind, refers to the part of our mind that operates below the level of conscious awareness. It contains a vast amount of information, memories, beliefs, emotions, and instincts that influence our thoughts, feelings, and behavior. The subconscious mind is constantly active and is responsible for automatic processes such as regulating bodily functions, storing and retrieving memories, and influencing our habits and reactions.

While the conscious mind represents our immediate awareness and rational thinking, the subconscious mind plays a significant role in shaping our long-term behavior, attitudes, and beliefs. It can also influence our dreams, creative thinking, and problem-solving abilities. The subconscious mind is often associated with intuitive insights, gut feelings, and the processing of information that occurs outside of conscious awareness.

It's important to note that the relationship between the conscious and subconscious mind is complex and interconnected. Information and experiences from the subconscious mind can influence our conscious thoughts and actions, and our conscious awareness can also affect the programming and functioning of the subconscious mind.

Understanding and harnessing the power of the subconscious mind can be beneficial for personal growth, self-improvement, and overcoming certain challenges or limiting beliefs. Techniques such as hypnosis, meditation, and affirmations are often used to access and work with the subconscious mind to promote positive changes in behavior and mindset.

# BENEFIT BY TAPPING INTO YOUR SUBCONSCIOUS MIND

Tapping into your subconscious mind can be a powerful tool for personal growth and self-improvement. I have studied this for years and years. Here are some awesome techniques that people use to access their own subconscious.

1) Meditation: Regular meditation can help you quiet your conscious mind and reach a state of relaxation where your subconscious thoughts and beliefs may become more accessible.

2) Visualization: Engaging in creative visualization exercises allows you to vividly imagine and create mental images of your goals, desires, and aspirations. This technique can help you connect with your subconscious mind and align it with your conscious intentions.

3) Affirmations: Repeating positive affirmations can help reprogram your subconscious mind by replacing negative thought patterns with empowering beliefs. Choose affirmations that resonate with you and repeat them regularly with conviction.

4) Hypnosis: Seeking the assistance of a trained hypnotherapist or using self-hypnosis techniques can help you bypass your conscious mind and access your subconscious directly. Under hypnosis, you can explore and address underlying beliefs, fears, or traumas.

5) Journaling: Writing in a journal, particularly in a free-flowing or stream-of-consciousness style, can reveal insights from your subconscious mind. By allowing your thoughts to flow onto paper without judgment or censorship, you may uncover hidden emotions, patterns, or ideas.

6) Dream analysis: Paying attention to your dreams and keeping a dream journal can provide valuable insights into your subconscious mind. Dreams often contain symbols and metaphors that can reflect your deepest thoughts, fears, and desires.

Remember that tapping into your subconscious mind requires patience, practice, and self-reflection. It's essential to approach these techniques with an open mind and a willingness to explore your inner self. Additionally, seeking guidance from a qualified professional, such as a therapist or coach, can offer personalized support on your journey of self-discovery.

## BECOME CONGRUENT IN YOUR THOUGHTS

Indeed, congruency is an important aspect when it comes to thoughts, beliefs, and actions. Congruency refers to the alignment or consistency between different elements within an individual's mindset and behavior. When there is congruency, there is harmony and coherence between what one thinks, says, and does.

In terms of thoughts, congruency implies that our beliefs, values, and perceptions are consistent with one another. When our thoughts are congruent, we experience a sense of integrity and clarity within our own mental framework. This internal consistency allows for a more stable and balanced perspective on life.

Furthermore, congruency extends to our actions and behaviors. It means that we align our actions with our beliefs and values. When our actions are congruent with our thoughts, we are more authentic and genuine in our interactions with others. This consistency fosters trust, as people can rely on us to act in accordance with what we profess to believe.

Congruency is also important for personal growth and self-awareness. When we identify any inconsistencies or in-congruencies within ourselves, it gives us an opportunity to reflect, reassess our beliefs, and make necessary adjustments. By striving for congruency, we can create a more coherent and integrated sense of self.

Overall, congruency in thoughts, beliefs, and actions helps us cultivate authenticity, integrity, and a stronger sense of self. It allows us to live in alignment with our values and fosters healthier relationships with others.

## TAP INTO YOUR SUBCONSCIOUS MIND
## FOR YOUR SUCCESS

Tap into your subconscious mind so that you can be the director of your life. Much like a director in Hollywood movies, you, too, can direct your thoughts to be in congruency with each other. This is the ultimate goal. Allow your subconscious mind to work 24 hours a day, even though you are not consciously focusing on it. It's very much like a muscle. You will need to practice and train your brain to create the harmony between your conscious and subconscious minds. Once you create this harmony, success starts to flow in every area of your life. It's your time to take control.

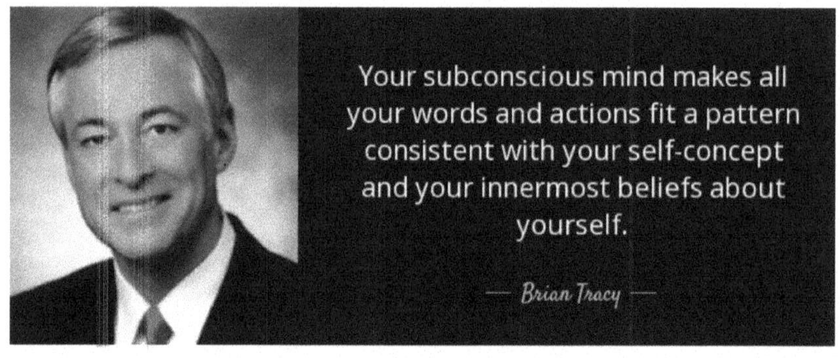

*DORIA CORDOVA*

# THE SUBCONSCIOUS—THE GREATEST POWER

I am so honored to be part of this publication—to have the privilege of writing about the "greatest power" for any human being, the Subconscious, and to share what I've learned in nearly five decades of personally working on myself.

Once we understand the potential benefits and drawbacks of the Subconscious and we have established firewalls and self-mastery tools to deal with it under any adverse circumstance, our level of confidence, self-trust, and self-mastery goes through the roof!

I know that I can support you in having greater success, personal power, prosperity, health, peace, and joy. I can help you to have a life where you can live in the greatest experience of them all: Sufficiency!

The Subconscious mind has been a topic of fascination and debate for centuries. It is widely known that our Subconscious thoughts and emotions play a significant role in shaping our decisions and relationships, especially in the business world... Everywhere we look!

Bottom line: The Subconscious has a huge influence on our lives. Allow me to offer practical guidance on overcoming these pitfalls, fostering greater conscious awareness, and enhancing the overall quality of important decisions.

To give you a little context as to why I have "earned the right" to speak about this subject, let me share a bit about my life. Through a series of wondrous circumstances that I consciously never imagined, I became part of the team of pioneers of the entrepreneurial, experiential, transformational training industry in the late 1970s which now permeates the industry globally. This field, of course, supports people around the world to clear their Subconscious and reach the life of their dreams.

Everyone's life is affected by Generalized Principles. A Generalized Principle is always true. These are principles proven by science and physics. Whether we believe in them or not, they exist. One Generalized Principle is **gravity**; another is **leverage**; and one not so well-known but equally powerful is **precession**. Precession is the physics term for ripple effects. They are always present.

The synergy that can be created when we understand how powerfully the Subconscious affects our thoughts, behaviors, feelings, and actions, and learn to manage it, is extraordinary.

At the young age of 26, through a spiritual awakening, and having attended one of the first (and most successful) human potential trainings, EST, I was blessed to learn at the time that if I couldn't have control over my circumstances (I had experienced the tremendous loss of my beloved, two miscarriages, and a dozen friends), at least I could have control of my consciousness.

I finally had a glimpse that I could have a life that could work for me with much less fear, anxiety, and stress... The possibilities were heavenly! I knew I could be financially successful. I just didn't know that I could also be personally happy and live a purpose-driven life.

Once I started putting my attention on clearing my Subconscious of negative programming, my life pivoted to what eventually led me to create the results that are evident today.

In the 1970s, there wasn't as much research as we have now. We now know that self-mastery work, exercise, breathing, healthy foods, a focus on adding value to others, being loving and kind, having integrity, and committing our lives to the betterment of humanity can bring us true happiness and joy.

As a Latina woman having accomplished the "American dream," I know that it had much to do with the values that were taught to me by my mother, auntie, grandmother, and other amazing family members that led my thinking.

And then there was the Subconscious...

I had to overcome strong beliefs, thoughts, and decisions that I had made because of my environment, as I had been literally "brainwashed" in traditional schools (as had everyone else). I had to learn Financial Literacy on my own by attending programs like the Burklyn Business School (which evolved to what I own today, the Excellerated Business School) and many programs taught by experts outside of traditional education.

I had to clear Subconscious blocks to achieve the level of success that I knew I had in me, and thank God, I realized that I actually had to raise my "deservability" level in order to allow more success, in every area of my life.

How did I do that? First, I am eternally thankful to Sondra Ray, one of the original metaphysicians who influenced many of the leaders in the industry, including myself. When I discovered that I wanted to commit myself to the betterment of humanity and attended the first business school for entrepreneurs of its kind that I mentioned earlier, all these negative thoughts began to literally spurt from my Subconscious. I found myself fighting beliefs that I literally didn't know I had.

She then introduced me to the *"Magical Exercises"* (a title that emerged after decades of personally using them, as many other leaders in our industry). I had to clear my Subconscious of the beliefs about money, business, and success that I had learned from my parents, family, school, church, books, movies, the environment—essentially, the world!

Most of humanity is programmed to believe that we live in a world of scarcity—even though the Malthusian theory of economics (the work of governments is to manage scarce resources) was proven obsolete in the early 1970s. Think about that… That was over 50 years ago! It was proven then that the world had enough resources to feed everyone, to house everyone.

The systems and tools were there to share energy sources for the world to have electricity, which is essential to eradicating poverty and hunger. We actually live in a world that has enough, yet sufficiency is one of the most fleeting experiences for so many!

If you don't believe that, your Subconscious is hard at work. And here's where the daily, moment-to-moment discipline comes into play: take three deep breaths. Feel the reaction, question what is being activated, and decide if (whatever you are feeling) is something that is worth working on so that you are the CEO of your life, and the captain of your ship. This will help you clearly and soberly make decisions that will empower you to have a successful life.

Recognize when you are in reaction. Take three deep breaths and come back to center. Do the work and find that inner family that can lead you to have more courage, more clarity, and more certainty than that which you choose, which will lead you to a better life.

I learned this very young: Just because I don't believe something, doesn't mean that it isn't true. Your beliefs will taint your reality, so that you will find the evidence necessary to make those beliefs true. You can actually see it in the division that has been created in the world today around medicine, science, and technology.

Who is running the show, you or your Subconscious? Are you aware of the beliefs that you have about the subject that you are tackling today? Do you have the correct information, facts, and what has worked in that situation? Are you willing to learn from other people's mistakes? Or are you the type that will spend the rest of your life having the same "learning experiences" (mistakes), hoping for a different outcome?

Do the *Magical Exercises* that have made a huge difference to so many who have done them. You can find them in our www.FridaysWithDoria.com global platform under *Resources*. Clear your Subconscious and do the daily work to create a reality that empowers you, that allows you to find the information, tools, and techniques that have worked for tens of millions to have a successful business, or organization (for-profit or non-profit).

Study those who have created extraordinary results in the area that you are interested in, or already have success in. Remember, there are **three stages of money: making it, keeping it, and growing it.** What stage are you in? Each stage requires for your Subconscious to have empowering beliefs every step of the way. It's the greatest power, after all.

If your Subconscious is running amok with beliefs that you have collected unchecked, you will have chaos. If you are aware of them and are CONSCIOUSLY working on them, you will have power.

"It is the Way," as they say in the *Mandalorian – Star Wars* offshoot.

Consciously increase your self-awareness. Developing a deeper understanding of your emotions, thoughts, and biases can help you recognize when they might be influencing your decision-making. Mindfulness meditation, journaling, and self-reflection exercises such as the *Magical Exercises* are effective ways to cultivate self-awareness.

I personally have practiced Transcendental Meditation (TM) for 14 years without fail. It has been one of my greatest disciplines, and here's why.

Once you begin to have self-mastery, you will find that your intuition (gut feeling) will become more prevalent... Your ability to process new information and experiences will lead you to insights that may not be immediately apparent through logical analysis. Intuition can be a valuable tool in making quick decisions or identifying potential opportunities and risks. My ability to make decisions has sped up and improved.

Your emotional intelligence will increase exponentially. You will find that certain situations that used to trigger you no longer do. Learn to manage your emotions effectively. Acknowledge and validate your emotions but avoid letting them dictate your decisions. Techniques such as emotional intelligence training, stress management, and seeking feedback from trusted mentors, colleagues, and friends can help you regulate your emotions and make more balanced decisions.

You will excel at identifying patterns and connections between seemingly unrelated pieces of information, which can lead to innovative ideas and solutions. You will have enhanced creativity. Many creative insights and ideas arise from the subconscious mind, often when we least expect them. This can lead to breakthroughs in problem-solving and the development of new products or strategies.

I recommend that you create environments that foster creativity in your business, organization, and family! Encourage brainstorming sessions, open discussions, and collaboration within your teams/family to stimulate the Subconscious mind and generate innovative ideas. Providing a safe space for experimentation and risk-taking can lead to breakthroughs in problem-solving.

Remember, the Subconscious mind wields significant influence over our business decisions and relationships. By understanding its origins and recognizing its potential benefits and drawbacks, we can develop strategies to harness its power and not only make better-informed decisions, we can also design our lives so that we actualize our most cherished heart's desires!

May the Force Be with You!

# DAME DORIA (DC) CORDOVA, PHD

## (HON.)

Dame Doria Cordova owns *Excellerated Business Schools® for Entrepreneurs* and *Money & You®*, a global organization that has over 165,000 participants for the past 42 years from over 85 countries, especially from Asia Pacific and the Americas. The programs are taught in English, Chinese, and Japanese–soon expanding to Tamil, Hindi, and other Indian languages–plus, Spanish, Bahasa, and more… Many of today's wealth and business leaders have attended the *Money & You* program and transformed the way they teach and run their organizations.

Through these graduates, including her business partnership of 9 years in the 80's and '90's with Robert T. Kiyosaki of *Rich Dad/Poor Dad* fame, Dame Cordova's work has touched the lives of millions all over the world. The essence of her work is to not only focus on the bottom line and profits but also to offer products and services that add value to humanity.

She is the only Latin woman that was part of the group of pioneers, led by Marshall Thurber and Bobbi DePorter of ***www.Supercamp.com***, that began the development of the transformational, experiential, entrepreneurial training industry. She inherited the work over 36 years ago which has now expanded to what it's today through countless partners, associates, teams, graduates and the support of many.

Along with Robert Kiyosaki, of the *Rich Dad/Poor Dad* series, in 1985 they opened that industry in Australia, New Zealand and later Singapore. Subsequently, along with new partners, the Malaysia, Taiwan, Hong Kong, China, Indonesia, India, Thailand, Philippines, Cambodia and other markets have been opened. Their larger market is in the Chinese language— having been in China for 19 years. Dr. Willson Lin and his team have put the programs "on the map". Her latest expansion of the work is the English ***Global Excellerated Business School for Entrepreneurs***. This global gathering of global social entrepreneurs will be held in Port Douglas, North Queensland, Australia on November 6 – 14, 2021

***wwwDCDoriaCordova.com***

# *CHAPTER 12*
# EVERYTHING IS LEARNABLE

*"The key to success is to focus our conscious mind
on things we desire not things we fear.
Everything is learnable, and what others have learned,
you can learn as well.
To earn more you must learn more. Our goal is not to change
everyone, but to change those that are
ready for change."*
**~ Brian Tracy**

Ladies and gentlemen and curious minds, allow me to share a perspective with you. I believe everything is learnable!

The brightest minds in history have all shown us that our brain power is much more powerful than our brawn power. It's also well known that each of these brilliant minds have all been considered 'crazy' as well. It's the crazy ones who take chances, risks, and try things who seem to make those breakthroughs and invent something innovative and contribute to the world for ever and ever.

Guess what? My theory is that everything is learnable. This is an amazing concept and means that if someone else had done it before you, you can do it, too!

There's a great story about a runner from England named Roger Bannister. In 1954, Roger was the very first person to ever run a sub-four-minute mile. He came in at 3 minutes and 59 seconds. This was huge. But, the huge part of the story was yet to come. He held his world record for exactly 46 days, until someone else beat it... and then another, and another. The moral of the story is that once people realized it was possible, they all started to train their brains. Just the mere realization that it was possible was enough for people to start breaking that threshold. They all started to keep these positive thoughts of victory in the forefront of their minds. It works!

## BENEFIT BY TAPPING INTO YOUR BRAIN POWER

Picture a classroom without walls, where the curriculum extends beyond textbooks and lectures. I believe that every experience, challenge, and encounter is a lesson waiting to be absorbed. From the intricacies of quantum physics to the nuances of human emotions, the canvas of learning is ever-expanding.

In the symphony of learning, no subject is too complex, no skill too elusive. As we traverse the landscape of knowledge, let us do so with the unwavering belief that everything is within our grasp. The realization of this concept opens up the doors to the world for all of us.

The brain plays a crucial role in our self-development, encompassing various cognitive processes, emotional regulation, and learning mechanisms.

## KEY FACTORS IN HOW THE BRAIN CONTRIBUTES TO SELF-DEVELOPMENT:

**1) Neuroplasticity:** The brain has the ability to reorganize itself by forming new neural connections throughout life. This process, known as neuroplasticity, allows individuals to adapt to experiences, learn new skills, and overcome challenges.

**2) Learning & Memory:** The brain's capacity to acquire, process, and store information is fundamental to self-development. Learning involves changes in synaptic connections, and memory allows individuals to retain and retrieve knowledge, experiences, and skills that contribute to personal growth.

**3) Emotional Regulation:** Different brain regions, such as the amygdala and prefrontal cortex, play crucial roles in emotional processing and regulation. Self-development often involves understanding and managing emotions, which relies on the brain's ability to regulate emotional responses and make informed decisions.

**4) Executive Functions:** The prefrontal cortex is associated with executive functions, including decision-making, planning, problem-solving, and impulse control. These functions are essential for setting goals, making choices, and navigating life in a purposeful manner.

**5) Social Cognition:** The brain is wired for social interactions, and self-development is closely tied to understanding oneself in the context of social relationships. Areas like the mirror neuron system contribute to empathy, understanding others, and developing social skills.

**6) Habit Formation:** The basal ganglia and other brain regions are involved in habit formation. Positive habits contribute to self-development by fostering discipline, consistency, and personal growth over time.

**7) Mindfulness & Reflection:** The brain's default mode network is associated with self-reflection and introspection. Practices like mindfulness and meditation can influence the brain's activity, promoting self-awareness and fostering personal development.

**8) Neurotransmitters & Mood:** Neurotransmitters, such as serotonin and dopamine, influence mood and motivation. Balancing these chemicals is crucial for maintaining a positive mindset, resilience, and the motivation necessary for self-improvement.

**9) Critical Periods & Sensitive Periods:** The brain is more plastic and adaptable during certain critical periods in development. Understanding these periods can guide efforts in self-development, emphasizing the importance of lifelong learning and personal growth.

Our brain's intricate network of neurons, synapses, and specialized regions collaborates to support self-development. Through neuroplasticity, learning, emotional regulation, and various cognitive processes, individuals can shape their thoughts, behaviors, and emotions to enhance their overall well-being and personal growth.

**Becoming a Student of Your Brain to Develop Better Habits**
Certainly! Building better habits involves understanding the underlying mechanisms of habit formation and implementing strategies to make positive behaviors more automatic. Here are some general tips to help you build better habits:

• **Start Small:** Begin with small, manageable changes. Gradually increase the difficulty as the habit becomes more ingrained.

• **Be Specific:** Clearly define the habit you want to develop. Instead of a vague goal like "exercise more," specify: "Go for a 20-minute walk every morning."

• **Set Clear Goals:** Establish clear and realistic goals. Break them down into short-term and long-term objectives.

• **Create a Routine:** Associate your new habit with an existing routine. For example, if you want to develop a reading habit, do it right after breakfast every day.

• **Use Triggers:** Identify triggers or cues that will remind you to perform the habit. This could be a specific time, place, or action.
• **Track Progress:** Keep a record of your efforts. Tracking your progress can be motivating and help you stay on course.

• **Stay Consistent:** Consistency is key when forming habits. Stick to your routine, even on days when motivation is low.

• **Celebrate Small Wins:** Acknowledge and celebrate your achievements along the way. This positive reinforcement can strengthen the habit loop.

• **Remove Barriers:** Make it easy to engage in the desired behavior. If your goal is to eat healthier, keep healthy snacks readily available.

• **Get Accountability:** Share your goals with someone who can provide support and hold you accountable. This could be a friend, family member, or a mentor.

• **Learn from Setbacks:** If you encounter setbacks, view them as learning opportunities rather than failures. Analyze what went wrong and adjust your approach.

• **Visualize Success:** Imagine yourself successfully completing the habit. Visualization can enhance motivation and commitment.

## TAP INTO YOUR BRAIN POWER TO GUIDE YOU FOR ULTIMATE SUCCESS

If you allow yourself to truly tap into your brain power, it will provide you a blueprint and guide for success. Your brain is more powerful than any man-made computer on the face of this earth. Use it wisely and use it often!

*JOHN ASSARAF*

# YOUR BRAIN & SELF-LIMITING BELIEFS

## THE GOOD, THE BAD, & THE UGLY

If no one had told you otherwise, would you believe that the Earth was flat, the stars were celestial beings, and beyond the horizon, the sea dropped off into oblivion?

If you're like most modern people, you have other ideas in mind.

A spherical Earth spins on an axis; the planets revolve around the Sun. Stars aren't gods of fire—they're luminous spheroids of plasma. If a crowd of people were to try to convince you otherwise, you'd have centuries of scientific evidence to prove them wrong.

But what if, when you woke up each morning, you assumed that nothing much existed beyond *your* horizon?

What if every time you saw yourself in the mirror, your reflection echoed back: "You're neither smart nor spectacular enough to succeed," "You're too unlucky to ever be loved"?

Would you let those beliefs prevent you from setting sail to see what truly lies on your horizon?

## TAKE 'EM TO TASK

Sadly, there's no peer-review in your head to fact check any ideas you may have of yourself. There's no objective eye in your prefrontal cortex to test the validity of the hypotheses you've formed about your life, the universe, and everything.

It's all too easy to turn conjectures into conclusions. Theories into dogma. Impressions into judgments.

A statement like "I'm worthless," "I'm unlovable," or "I'm doomed to failure" might sound harmless if you say it once. But words have a way of persuading even unbelievers you repeat them often enough. You may find yourself cherry-picking memories from your personal history to prove to yourself that the beliefs you hold in the present are true.

Call it negative self-talk. Self-flagellation. The devil on your shoulder. None of us have escaped the clutches of self-limiting beliefs. They creep up when we're about to step out of our comfort zone. They may pull us into cowardice when we feel brave enough to follow a dream. They often lurk below the field of awareness, which makes them even more insidious.

Scientists have been trained to scrutinize any theory they have about the universe.

Isn't it time to take your negative self-talk to task?

## WHAT THE BLEEP'S BEHIND A BELIEF?

What goes on in your brain when you believe—in a benevolent creator of the universe, in life-after-death, or in damnation for that matter? Why, from the perspective of the evolution of cognition, do human beings form belief systems—like religion—in the first place?

Social scientists ask why cultures transmit systems of belief: Why do native Polynesians see spirits in the waves and Catholics feel certain of the Holy Trinity? Biologists see beliefs as traits of evolution: Which social and emotional interactions have led to their formation?

To neuroscientists, beliefs run deeper than the culture or the social and environmental contexts. They represent complex brain-based phenomena that form the basis of all social exchanges and moral intuitions.

## THE GOOD

When you trust in the goodness of your neighbors, it enables you to participate in community life, and to form healthy social bonds. Without community, you might find it difficult to thrive, let alone survive, in the world. Unless your neighbors prove otherwise, it's healthy for your brain to believe that they're decent people.

Moreover, a belief in karma, or "what goes around comes around," also encourages neighbors to act ethically towards each other. Codes of behavior, at their best, help people to live in relative peace.

## THE BAD

Beliefs also offer people a way to cope when difficult things happen in life. They help humans to accept misfortune. If you grow up with a cat, and that cat gets hit by a bus, it's comforting to believe in an animal heaven. When a volcano erupts, a belief in a just but fiery god can help people to make sense of devastation.

## THE UGLY

Along the same lines, when you say to yourself, "I'm unworthy," your brain might be looking for an easy way to make sense of personal misfortune. Although the human brain is a complex and intricately fascinating organ—it's also lazy. If your brain can operate with minimal effort, it will. Thinking that you're unworthy of love may be the quickest pathway your brain has found to protect you from the losses and disappointments inherent in intimate human relationships.

## WHERE IN THE BRAIN IS BELIEF?

Some neuroscientists hypothesize that specific patterns of brain activity play different roles in the art of believing. Some beliefs engage posterior regions of the brain while others engage areas involved in abstract reasoning. Whenever you believe anything about yourself—whether it's "I'm a mess" or "I'm the best thing since sliced bread," you engage brain networks involved in memory retrieval and imagery.

The default mode network, or what some researchers call "the imagination network," plays a central role in formulating and maintaining beliefs about who you think you are. It's the network that governs all your autobiographical memories. It daydreams about who you might have been in the past and who you think you might be in the future.

The more you recall ideas and feelings about yourself, the stronger the neural pathways that carry those memories will get. That process is what forms your self-concept; it's what builds your identity. Freud referred to the whole thing as the "ego."

Whatever you call it, a consistent belief in who you are as a person also has an evolutionary purpose. Without a stable sense of self, life would be a helluva thing to navigate.

## AYE, THERE'S THE RUB

Now, this may be hard to believe—but every belief you have about yourself is "self-limiting."

Do you believe that you are good? Bad? Ugly?

Whatever you believe and however you believe it, you're putting limits around who you truly are. As Shakespeare's Hamlet says in Act 2, Scene 2: "There is nothing either good or bad, but thinking makes it so."

If you think you are a "good" person, that belief may be preventing you from appreciating the full spectrum of your personality. Believing in your unassailable goodness can lead to all forms of denial. But if you believe yourself to be a "bad" person, is it any better?

## WHAT'S THE SOLUTION: INNERCISE!

Train your brain to keep those self-limiting beliefs from running wild and unverified in your mind. Just as you wouldn't drink milk past its due date, don't swallow ideas about yourself just because they're sitting on the front shelf of your brain!

You exercise your leg muscles when you walk an extra mile. Now walk an extra mile in your mind. Innercise the "muscles" (or synapses) that form your neural pathways, so they remain agile, responsive, and awake.

Expand your potential for deeper levels of awareness. Whenever your default mode network starts stirring up beliefs about who you think you are, notice those beliefs for what they are.

But first, take a moment and notice the pattern of your breathing. Is it quick? Soft? Labored?

Whatever you're experiencing, let go of any judgment.

Notice your physical body in the present. If it helps, gently caress the palms of your hands. Experience pleasure, without judgment, blame, shame, guilt, or justification, in this moment. Let go of any beliefs of who you think you might be right now. If beliefs arise, just notice them dispassionately.

When you feel relaxed and steady in your body and mind, tap into your wise inner voice (or your expert innerciser if you prefer).

Ask your expert innerciser: What beliefs do I harbor about myself that are reigning in my true self? Are any of my beliefs holding me back from living fully? Are any of my ideas about who I am inhibiting me from meeting my potential? From reaching my goals?

Write down those beliefs.

Now read them back. Slowly. Calmly.

Recognize that whatever you're reading is something you've taken part in constructing. It's all fabrication. And if it's limiting you now, you have the power to let the story go.

When you achieve a little distance from those self-limiting beliefs, recognize and relish in having freedom from them. The more you do this, the more it will become a habit and the more natural it will feel to sit in the driver's seat in front of an open road.

In this space of freedom, it's your call. It's your turn. Hands on the wheel.

Choose to believe something new about yourself. Go down a different road. Play a different part in your own life. Believe in your self-worth, your beauty, your potential. Whatever you wish.

Do you believe that you can meet your financial goals this year? Why not? What's holding you back? Is it something tangible? Can you name the limitations you're putting on your financial freedom? Write those barriers down and see them for what they are.

Do the same for any goal you may have, whether it's love or work or travel. Check in next week as we tackle the neuroscience of goal setting and achievement.

Now that you know a little bit more about what self-limiting beliefs are, isn't it easier to just sail past them?

# JOHN ASSARAF

---

John Assaraf, *"The Brain Whisperer,"* is one of the leading high-performance success coaches in the world. He is a behavioral neuroscience researcher who has appeared numerous times on Larry King Live, Anderson Cooper, and The Ellen DeGeneres Show.

As CEO and co-founder, he grew Re/Max of Indiana from a startup to 85 offices and 1200 sales associates who sold over $4 billion a year.

John was also one of the founders of Bamboo/IPIX, which went public on NASDAQ with a market cap of $2.5 billion.

John has written four books, including two New York Times bestsellers, that have been translated into 35 languages. He is the creator of the "Innercise" movement and has been featured in 11 movies, including the blockbuster hit *The Secret* and *Quest For Success* with Richard Branson and the Dalai Lama.

He lives in San Diego with his wife and two sons. In addition to being a vegan, meditator, an avid skier, and ocean lover, he loves traveling the world and making some of the tastiest hot sauces using some of the hottest peppers on the planet.

**Today, he is CEO of MyNeuroGym.com,** a neuroscience-based company, dedicated to helping individuals strengthen their mindset, so they achieve their goals and dreams… faster and easier than ever before.

*www.JohnAssaraf.com*

# CHAPTER 13

# THE 90% FORMULA ~ NOT JUST A HUNCH

*"Through the aid of the sixth sense, you will be warned of impending dangers in time to avoid them, and notified of opportunities in time."*
~ Napoleon Hill

Wow, what an amazing journey this has been! I am so honored and blessed to have been surrounded by so many fantastic leaders from around the world in sharing principles, stories, and lessons of success.

It all started when I was nineteen years old. I started studying Dr. Wayne Dyer's works, which led me on a journey I would embrace with open arms. Through this journey, I always knew I would learn how to be successful, and I also always knew I had a gift for seeing things in a positive light.

I never knew this thought pattern or hunch that I was feeling throughout my life was actually a thing. I never knew it was studied by the greats before me. I never knew people could actually learn to harness this strategy and make it a habit. I never knew it was called the 'sixth sense.'

We all have the ability to create our own magic in our lives by learning how to use this sixth sense, which Napoleon Hill refers to as the creative imagination. Hill believed that our creative imagination is the key to tapping into infinite intelligence, a source of knowledge and wisdom that exists beyond our conscious mind.

## WHAT IS THE SIXTH SENSE?

There are so many benefits in harnessing the habit of our sixth sense. But, before we dive into the benefits, let's discuss what it actually is first. There are many definitions and interpretations of what our sixth sense is. My definition is simple. My sixth sense is when I harness that internal feeling or knowing. It's when I can feel a hunch of what is to come next. It's believing in yourself when your brain tells you that you should be careful of what is to come and pay attention to it.

Have you ever just had a hunch of feeling about something in advance? That is your sixth sense in action. And many of us look back and say something like, "I knew I should have listened to my gut feeling."

I highly recommend that you observe those feelings from now on. Put the attention to it that it deserves. You will thank me for doing so. Hill believed that successful people trust their intuitions and hunches, and that acting on intuition can help transform thoughts into physical reality. He also believed that people should seize opportunities when they present themselves. Successful people listen to their gut feelings and pay attention to their hunches. The sixth sense is the ability to perceive something that is not normally accessible to the five common senses that we all have.

## BENEFITS OF CREATING MAGIC WITH YOUR SIXTH SENSE

There are so many benefits to using your sixth sense. It's kind of like a superhero power we can all possess. Think about it. What if I told you that you could trust your intuition and feelings about something, and you would be correct? What a tremendous benefit in making decisions. This habit would also save you so much time in your life.

## MY SIXTH SENSE IN ACTION

I have seen my sixth sense work for me in so many areas of my life. What an absolute blessing it is to be able to harness this. I started to realize that my sixth sense was showing up more throughout my days. I decided to start testing my theory and see if it truly works. I started keeping a record of how I used my sixth sense and to see if I was correct in doing so. Wow! Can I just tell you how amazing the results were?

I started to call my sixth sense by a nickname I would give it. It is now called my "90% Formula."

## THE 90% FORMULA

So, what exactly is my 90% formula? Once I started to record each time I had a hunch, a gut feeling, or a sixth sense about something, I started to see that I was correct most of the time. But, I really wanted to test it and see how accurate it was and how many times I was accurate in my choice. After years of recording my results, the results came out to about 90% of the time. That's right! My accuracy rate is 90% of the time. WOW. This truly is a superpower in my mind.

I started to use it all of the time. In fact, I don't go a day without actually implementing this new superpower habit of mine. I highly recommend you do the same. I mean, think about it. If I could tell you that simply by following your own gut feeling, you will succeed in your decision to be the right one 90% of the time, wouldn't you harness this as well? You can!

Simply make that decision to do so. Take action right now and be disciplined about it. Each time you come to a crossroads in a decision-making factor, think about it, ask yourself what your gut feeling really is, and act upon that feeling in that direction. Yes, it's as simple as that. You're welcome!

## LIVE BY YOUR GUT

Decide today to live by your gut feelings. Our bodies are created for ultimate success. This includes your brain power. This also includes your internal feelings. These are innate abilities we all are born with. It's time for you to tap into this superpower and harness the habit of your sixth sense.

## TAP INTO YOUR SIXTH SENSE NOW

It's time for you to tap into this newfound habit. It's time for you to create magic in your life. It's time for you to take control of your results and your success. It's YOUR time!

*KEVIN HARRINGTON*

# MASTERING INTUITIVE DECISION-MAKING

For over forty years, I've built, invested in, and scaled businesses worldwide. You might know me from the television show, *Shark Tank,* or perhaps from my role in creating the modern infomercial. Through these ventures and countless others, I've refined my decision-making process to the point where I can often rely on a feeling—an instinctual sense—to guide me in the split second it takes to decide whether an opportunity is worth pursuing. That instinct is what Napoleon Hill calls the "sixth sense" in *Think and Grow Rich.* It's not something I had when I first started, but over the years, I've developed this ability, this "entrepreneurial radar," through trial, error, and intentional practice.

The sixth sense isn't a mystical force; it's the culmination of knowledge, experience, and quick analysis—the subconscious mind applying what you know and feel in the moment. It's an edge; when you're in business, that edge can mean the difference between a missed opportunity and a multimillion-dollar success. This is the most challenging trait for people to learn and obtain because it involves a gut feeling and developing the sense through all of the other steps in this process.

Today, I'll share how I developed my sixth sense in business, the process I use to make rapid, accurate decisions, and the key lessons I've learned that you can apply in your own journey toward mastering intuitive decision-making.

## DEVELOPING THE SIXTH SENSE

When I was starting out as a young entrepreneur in the 1980s, I didn't have what you'd call a sixth sense. I was just trying to get a foothold in the industry. My journey began with a $25,000 investment in Quantum International, which eventually became a $500-million-a-year business listed on the New York Stock Exchange. That success didn't happen overnight, nor did my sense for evaluating risk and opportunity. But with time and experience, I found myself developing a deeper, almost automatic intuition.

In business, I have been pitched thousands upon thousands of ideas. In fact, over a decade after *Shark Tank*, I still receive about a thousand pitches a month. This is where my sixth sense has truly been refined. On *Shark Tank*, contestants had just three minutes to sell their concept, and I had three minutes to decide if I wanted to invest potentially millions of dollars. There wasn't time for in-depth due diligence. I had to rely on my gut and make fast decisions, which were often based on what I've come to know as my sixth sense.

# THE FOUNDATION: THE TEN-STEP PROCESS

Early in my career, I realized that a clear set of criteria could bolster my intuition. So, I began documenting the qualities I looked for in a potential product or business idea. Over time, I identified ten core factors that I could quickly evaluate. These were things like market potential, the uniqueness of the solution, scalability, and the ability to reach a mass audience. I would go down this list mentally, sometimes even subconsciously, checking off points as I listened to a pitch.

For instance, in a pitch, I look for a clear "tease" or problem that catches attention immediately. Then, there's the "please," where the solution is presented, showing how this product can meet a real need or deliver value. Finally, there's the "seize," where the offer becomes irresistible. If I could see these elements in a pitch and if it ticked enough of my ten boxes, that's when I knew I had something.

## AN EXAMPLE OF THE SIXTH SENSE IN ACTION: THE GREAT WOK OF CHINA

One of the best examples of my sixth sense in action is the story of the Chinese wok. About 35 years ago, I took my team to a trade show to scout potential products. We divided up the convention floor, and after a few hours, my team returned empty-handed, thinking the show had been a dud. But I'd found something—a hand-hammered wok made in mainland

China. It was unique, with ridges that cooked food differently and more efficiently.

My team was skeptical; they couldn't see the potential. "You can get a wok for $10 at Walmart," they said. But they didn't listen to the story behind it. This was no ordinary wok—it was authentic, hand-hammered in a way that brought out the best flavors in the food. I trusted my gut, invested in it, and spent $3,500 to create an infomercial. That product, marketed as "The Great Wok of China," went on to make $250 million in sales. This was my sixth sense at work, and it was only possible because I was open to seeing the opportunity where others saw none.

## LEARNING FROM EXPERIENCE

Think of it as a muscle that gets stronger over time. The more pitches I heard, the more products I evaluated, the sharper my instincts became. And the more I documented what worked and what didn't, the more I learned to trust my own judgment. This is why I encourage entrepreneurs to pay attention to the signals, document what they learn, and refine their approach.

Over time, I learned to dig deeper, read between the lines, and anticipate potential roadblocks. Sometimes, it's not just about what the person says but how they say it. Are they confident? Are they passionate? Do they believe in what they're selling? These intangible factors contribute to that sixth sense, helping me quickly assess whether something is worth my time and investment.

# TRUSTING YOUR GUT, BUT BACKING IT WITH RESEARCH

Having a sixth sense is essential, but so is balancing it with a dose of reality. Even with solid instincts, I never make decisions based on feeling alone. It's always backed by research and quick verification whenever possible. Early in my career, I would often rush into decisions based on excitement or eagerness alone. While that can sometimes work, it's also costly when it doesn't. I've learned that developing a solid sixth sense in business doesn't mean abandoning caution—it means having the foresight to gather supporting evidence even when time is limited.

Let's take *Shark Tank* as an example again. During those three-minute pitches, I would get an immediate feeling about a product or idea. But instead of solely relying on that gut feeling, I'd ask targeted questions to verify my instincts: "Who's the competition? What's the profit margin? Do you have any testimonials?" By digging into key areas, I could quickly confirm or adjust my initial impression. That's an essential lesson for anyone developing their sixth sense: use it as a guide, but don't ignore the value of facts and verification.

In another instance, I remember being pitched a product that initially seemed like a clear winner. It was flashy, unique, and had a solid story. My instincts were saying "Yes," but something felt off about the numbers. After a bit more digging, I discovered some financial inconsistencies that would have made it a much riskier investment than I'd thought. My gut was still right about the product's potential, but that extra research saved me from a potentially huge financial pitfall.

## THE "TEASE, PLEASE, & SEIZE" FRAMEWORK

One of my go-to approaches in making rapid evaluations is what I call the "Tease, Please, and Seize" framework. This is a process I've used to quickly assess and enhance any pitch or idea. It's a simple concept, but it's highly effective, especially when time is short.

**1. Tease:** This is the attention-grabber. Every product needs a clear, compelling hook that immediately captures the audience's interest. It's the "why should I care" factor. In a pitch, I look for something that stands out, whether it's a unique problem being solved or a captivating story.

**2. Please:** This step is about building trust and demonstrating value. I want to see proof. How does this product solve the problem? What benefits does it provide, and what is its unique selling point? Testimonials, endorsements, or evidence of effectiveness are crucial here.

**3. Seize:** Finally, this is the close, the irresistible offer. Every successful pitch should end with an opportunity that feels too good to pass up. Whether it's a limited-time deal, a free bonus, or a clear call to action, this is the part that pushes people to commit.

In my business, I've seen this process work time and time again, and it's something I instinctively apply when making quick decisions. For example, when evaluating a product on *Shark Tank*, I'd mentally run through the Tease, Please, and Seize steps to see if the entrepreneur was hitting each point effectively. If they could capture my attention, build credibility, and then close with a strong offer, they had my attention—and often, my investment.

## THE TEN KEY STEPS TO CREATING YOUR PERFECT PITCH

While the "Tease, Please, and Seize" framework offers a quick, effective way to assess and enhance pitches, I've developed a detailed process for delivering a perfect pitch over my career. This process builds on capturing attention, demonstrating value, and making an irresistible offer by breaking each aspect into focused steps. Here are my **10 Steps to Creating the Perfect Pitch** when evaluating the thousands of pitches I receive and making the best business decisions:

**1. Tease:** Begin by "hooking" your audience. Present the problem in a relatable and attention-grabbing way to make your audience recognize the need for a solution.

**2. Please:** Describe how your product or service uniquely solves the problem introduced in the Tease step. Highlight its main features, benefits, and value.

**3. Show in Action:** Demonstrate the product in real-time, showcasing its multi-functionality to add value and prove it can deliver on its promise.

**4. Add Value with "But Wait, There's More!":** Offer additional incentives or bonuses to make the deal more appealing and emphasize why it's a no-brainer investment.

**5. Provide Rock-Solid Testimonials:** Share credible third-party endorsements (such as user, professional, or celebrity testimonials) to build trust and social proof and make your solution more persuasive.

**6. Highlight Research & Competitive Analysis:** Show you've done the groundwork, understand the competition, and know why your solution is uniquely positioned.

**7. Reveal Your Dream Team:** Introduce a qualified team to support your venture, which will reassure investors about the project's potential for success.

**8. Explain Why You Need the Money:** Detail how the funds will be used, why they're necessary, and how they'll drive the business forward, making it clear you have a well-thought-out plan.

**9. Outline Your Marketing Plan:** Present a structured strategy for reaching your target audience, generating buzz, and scaling, demonstrating that you have a clear path to market.

**10. Ask for the Money:** End with a strong call to action. Ask for the funding, equity, or commitment you need, making the offer irresistible and easy to say "yes" to.

These ten steps aren't just about following a formula; they're designed to develop and strengthen your intuitive ability to pitch effectively. By internalizing these steps, you'll refine your sixth sense for recognizing opportunities and cultivate a clear, repeatable process to capture investor interest and close deals with confidence.

## NAVIGATING THE CHALLENGES OF PREJUDGMENT

One of the biggest challenges with the sixth sense is avoiding prejudgment. It's easy to fall into the trap of thinking you know everything about a product or person at first glance, but the sixth sense is about understanding beyond the surface. This was the case with the Great Wok of China, where I saw value others overlooked.

Prejudgment can kill opportunities, especially in a fast-paced environment. That's why I always recommend checking in with your sixth sense and asking yourself, "Am I giving this a fair chance, or am I making assumptions?" This habit has opened doors for me that might have otherwise remained closed, and it's an essential part of building a successful career in any field.

# BUILDING YOUR SIXTH SENSE OVER TIME

Developing a sixth sense doesn't happen overnight. It's a process built on years of learning, documenting, and honing your instincts. Like musicians practice scales until they can play by ear, entrepreneurs practice decisions until they can "hear" the right choice. My journey as an entrepreneur, from launching Quantum International to scaling twenty businesses to $100 million each, taught me that repetition and refinement are essential to building this ability.

For example, in the early days of my career, I took on nearly every opportunity that came my way. I wanted to gain experience and learn as much as I could. But as my intuition sharpened, I became more selective. Now, I can recognize patterns much faster, and my sixth sense often picks up on cues that others might miss. This has allowed me to make decisions more confidently and quickly, freeing up time and resources for new ventures.

For anyone reading this, if you want to build your own sixth sense, reflect on past choices to identify successful patterns. Reflect on your past successes and failures, identify patterns, and use those insights to inform your future choices. With each decision, you'll better recognize what feels right and be more adept at trusting your intuition.

# THE ROLE OF MENTORSHIP & A DREAM TEAM

While developing a sixth sense is essential, it's equally important to surround yourself with people who can complement and challenge your instincts. Throughout my career, I've benefited from having a "dream team" of experts, advisors, and mentors who bring diverse perspectives and insights to the table. Even the best intuition can benefit from an outside opinion, and having a trusted circle allows you to double-check your gut reactions with those you respect.

When I feel strongly about an opportunity, I often consult with other experts, asking them to play devil's advocate or give their honest take. Sometimes, a different perspective can illuminate potential risks or advantages that I hadn't considered. This helps me refine my sixth sense even further and provides a valuable safety net that I rely on to ensure I make the best decision possible.

Take the early days of *Shark Tank*, for example. We Sharks all have unique strengths and perspectives, and I often learned from how others approached a pitch. Watching Mark Cuban or Barbara Corcoran assess a deal with their own intuitive processes added to my toolkit and helped me see things from angles I hadn't previously considered. Developing a sixth sense is a personal journey, but input from a strong, diverse team can take it to new heights.

# TRUSTING YOUR SIXTH SENSE

Intuition is an invaluable skill that takes time to develop but pays dividends in the long run. You can develop a sixth sense that guides you through your professional journey by tuning in to your own experiences, listening to your instincts, and backing them up with thoughtful research.

As Napoleon Hill wrote, the sixth sense is the final step in the journey toward mastering the mind. For me, this journey has spanned over four decades, thousands of pitches, and billions in sales. Each decision, each pitch, and each success has contributed to this intuitive ability, allowing me to make impactful choices quickly and effectively. But I've also learned that trusting this sixth sense means listening to the stories behind products, resisting snap judgments, and relying on a strong team for insights and validation.

So, as you embark on your own journey to develop the sixth sense, remember to trust your instincts, seek out mentors, and be open to the stories that might lead to your next big success. This is the art and science of intuitive decision-making, and in today's fast-paced business world, it's more essential than ever.

# KEVIN HARRINGTON

Kevin Harrington is a pioneering entrepreneur and business leader with over four decades of experience. As one of the original "Sharks" on the Emmy-winning television show *Shark Tank*, Harrington has become a recognized authority in entrepreneurship, investing, and brand building. Known as the inventor of the infomercial and the "As Seen On TV" brand, Kevin revolutionized direct-to-consumer marketing, creating a global phenomenon that changed the way products are sold. He co-founded the Electronic Retailers Association (ERA). He was a founding board member of the Entrepreneurs' Organization (EO), which has grown to thousands of members across 45 countries, generating over $500 billion in member sales.

Kevin began his career in the early 1980s by investing $25,000 to launch Quantum International. This venture eventually generated $500 million annually on the New York Stock Exchange, driving its stock price from $1 to $20 per share. His next endeavor, HSN Direct, was a joint venture with the Home Shopping Network that generated hundreds of millions in sales. Throughout his career, Kevin has launched over 20 businesses that have surpassed $100 million in sales each and has introduced more than 500 products worldwide, amassing over $5 billion in total revenue.

Currently, Kevin operates a private consulting firm, leveraging his expertise to help companies expand distribution, strategize digital and media marketing, and build powerful celebrity partnerships. He is known for his ability to multiply the stock prices of companies he advises, and his influence has reached millions across various media platforms, including *The Wall Street Journal*, *Forbes*, *Inc.*, *USA Today*, and *CNBC*. As an author, Kevin shares his insights in bestselling books such as *Act Now: How I Turn Ideas into Million Dollar Products* and *Put a Shark in Your Tank*, as well as *the Secrets of Closing the Sale Master Class*, inspired by Zig Ziglar.

Kevin is one of the fan favorites at all of the Habitude Warrior Conferences. Kevin's enduring legacy in the entrepreneurial world combines his keen business acumen with an unmatched passion for innovation, making him one of today's most respected business mentors and thought leaders.

***www. KevinHarrington.tv***

# THE 13 FEATURED CELEBRITY AUTHORS

**DENIS WAITLEY** ~ Author of *Psychology of Winning & The NEW Psychology of Winning—Top Qualities of a 21st Century Winner*, NASA's Performance Coach, Featured in *The Secret*. ~ www.DenisWaitley.com

**SHARON LECHTER** ~ 5 Time N.Y. Times Bestselling Author. Author of *Think and Grow Rich for Women*, Co-Author of *Exit Rich, Rich Dad Poor Dad, Three Feet from Gold, Outwitting the Devil* and *Success and Something Greater.* ~ www.SharonLechter.com

**JIM CATHCART**~ Bestselling Author of Relationship Selling and The Acorn Principle, among many others. Certified Speaking Professional (CSP) and Former President of the National Speakers Association (NSA).
~ www.Cathcart.com

**MICHAEL E. GERBER** ~ N.Y. Times Bestseller of the mega-bestselling theory for over two consecutive decades...*The E-Myth* Books.
~ www.MichaelEGerberCompanies.com

**ERIK SWANSON** ~ 33 Time #1 International Bestselling Author, Award-Winning Speaker, Featured on TEDx Talks and Amazon Prime TV. Founder & CEO of the Habitude Warrior Brand. ~ www.SpeakerErikSwanson.com

**MARIE DIAMOND** ~ Featured in *The Secret*, Modern Day Spiritual Teacher, Inspirational Speaker, Feng Shui Master. ~ www.MarieDiamond.com

**DAN CLARK** ~ Award Winning Speaker, Speaker Hall of Fame, N.Y. Times Bestselling Author of *The Art of Significance.* ~ www.DanClark.com

**ALEC STERN** ~ America's Startup Success Expert, Co-Founder of Constant Contact, Speaker, Mentor, and Investor.
~ www.AlecSpeaks.com

**BRIAN TRACY** ~ International Bestselling Author and Motivational Speaker. Renowned Entrepreneur and Mentor to millions in the Speaking world. ~ www.BrianTracy.com

**LORAL LANGEMEIER** ~ 5 Time N.Y. Times Bestselling Author, Featured in *The Secret*, Author of *The Millionaire Maker* and *YES! Energy - The Equation to Do Less, Make More.* ~ www.LoralLangemeier.com

**DORIA CORDOVA** ~ CEO of Money & You, Excellerated Business School, Global Business Developer, Ambassador of New Education.
~ www.FridaysWithDoria.com

**JOHN ASSARAF** ~ Chairman & CEO NeuroGym, MrNeuroGym.com, New York Times bestselling author of *Having It All, Innercise,* and *The Answer.* Also featured in *The Secret.* ~ www.JohnAssaraf.com

**KEVIN HARRINGTON** ~ Original "Shark" on the hit TV show Shark Tank, Creator of the Infomercial, Pioneer of the As Seen on TV brand, Co-Author of Mentor to Millions. ~ www.KevinHarrington.TV

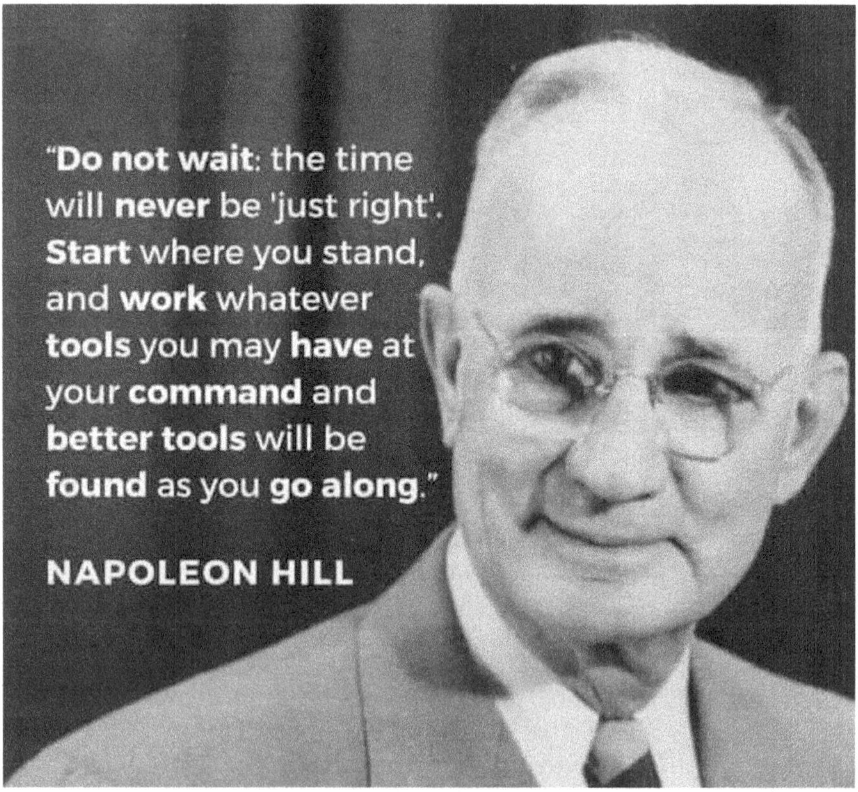

# ABOUT INTEGRITY PUBLISHING INTERNATIONAL

Integrity Publishing International is one of the world's most trusted hybrid publishing houses, dedicated to helping authors share their stories with authenticity, excellence, and integrity. Founded by Erik "Mr. Awesome" Swanson, a 33-Time #1 Bestselling Author, international speaker, and award-winning mentor, Integrity Publishing has guided more than 500 authors to achieve #1 Bestseller status in over 13 countries—and continues to empower writers across the globe.

Our mission is simple: to help you publish your story and become the author you were meant to be. Whether you're a first-time writer or a seasoned professional, our hands-on, step-by-step publishing programs make it easy to bring your message to life. With our Half Pack, Full Pack, and Ultimate Pack programs, authors can publish eBook, paperback, hardcover, and even audiobook formats—distributed through over 45,000 booksellers worldwide, including Amazon and Barnes & Noble.

Integrity Publishing is proud to offer more than publishing—we provide mentorship, community, and world-class resources to help every author shine. Our Authors Resource Page, ongoing training, and editorial support ensure your voice is heard, your story is polished, and your impact is global.

Led by an extraordinary team of professionals, our Founder Erik Swanson puts 1000% trust in his Managing Team Leader, Jon Kovach Jr. and our awesome Integrity Pub Team —we are committed to serving authors with heart, purpose, and excellence.

Join the hundreds of voices who have become #1 Bestselling Authors with Integrity Publishing International.

Your story matters. Let's share it with the world.

Team@IntegrityPub.com

IntegrityPublishingInternational.com

# *BECOME AN AUTHOR!*
# *JOIN THE 13 STEPS TO RICHES MOVEMENT*

Have you ever considered becoming an Author? Do you have a burning desire to share your stories and brilliance, but maybe you're like most people in the world and have no idea where to even start!

We are so excited to have created the ever-so-popular book series, *The 13 Steps To Riches*, based on the principles we learned from the one and only Napoleon Hill. This series includes some of Erik Swanson's close celebrity friends who share real-life and modern strategies for success.

It's YOUR time! Reach out to us to find out more about becoming a bestselling, published author with your beautiful photo on the cover while including your chapters inside the book. It will be a book literally branded to YOU!

Align yourself with some of the most powerful, influential, and respected leaders in the self-development world!

Reach out to our team at: *Team@IntegrityPub.com*

Kevin Harrington & Erik Swanson

Erik Swanson & Rita Davenport

**Erik Swanson & Dr. Joe Vitale**

**Erik Swanson & Les Brown**

**Stedman Graham & Erik Swanson**

**Erik Swanson & Bob Proctor**

**Erik Swanson speaking at World's Greatest Motivators**

**Erik Swanson & Mentor Brian Tracy**

**CEO Space Founder Berny Dohrmann
& Erik Swanson**

**Make A Wish Foundation Founder
Frank Shankwitz & Erik Swanson**

Erik Swanson & Sharon Lechter
& Habitude Warrior Speakers

Erik Swanson & Greg Reid

**Sharon Lechter & Erik Swanson**

Alec Stern & Erik Swanson

Alec Stern & Erik Swanson

Frank Shankwitz, Erik Swanson, Actor Andrew Steel

Erik Swanson & Jim Cathcart

**The Great Legend Jim Rohn & Erik Swanson**

**Erik Swanson & Greg Reid**

**Jack Canfield & Erik Swanson**

**Jon Kovach Jr. & Erik Swanson**

**Erik Swanson & Tom Hopkins**

**Erik Swanson & Pictionary Inventor Rob Angel**

**Jeffrey Gitomer & Erik Swanson**

**Erik Swanson & his FIRST Boss Duane Hendrickson**

**Actor Glenn Morshower & Erik Swanson**

**Leaders Dinner with Erik Swanson**

**Frank Shankwitz, Erik Swanson & Dr. Denis Waitley**

**Bill Walsh & Erik Swanson**

**Erik Swanson & Brian Tracy**
**(My first day working for Brian!)**

**Erik Swanson & Brian Tracy**

**2012 CNN Man of the Year Sir Bruno Serato,
Erik Swanson & Bob Donnell**

**Dr. Denis Waitley & Erik Swanson**

**Erik Swanson & Loral Langemeier**

Erik Swanson, Sharon Lechter, Michael Lechter,, Mark Victor Hansen, Crystal Dwyer Hansen, Sean Kanan,

**David Corbin & Erik Swanson**

**UGG Boots Founder Brian Smith & Erik Swanson**

Erik Swanson & John Gray

Erik Swanson & Jerry 'The Beaver" Mathers

**My Boys "SAMMY & LOUIE"**

**They love dressing up in their tuxedos!**

**Erik Swanson Loving Life!**

**Sharon Lechter & Erik Swanson**

**Tom Hopkins & Erik Swanson**

**Erik Swanson & Bob Donnell**

**Sharon Lechter, Nathan Barkocy, Erik Swanson**

HABITUDE WARRIOR
INFLUENCERS
A publication of
Success Profiles Magazine
Spring 2020
Erik
Swanson
How Do You
Define Success?
Strategies To
Raise Your Game
33 Top Influencers
To Watch In 2020
Amanda

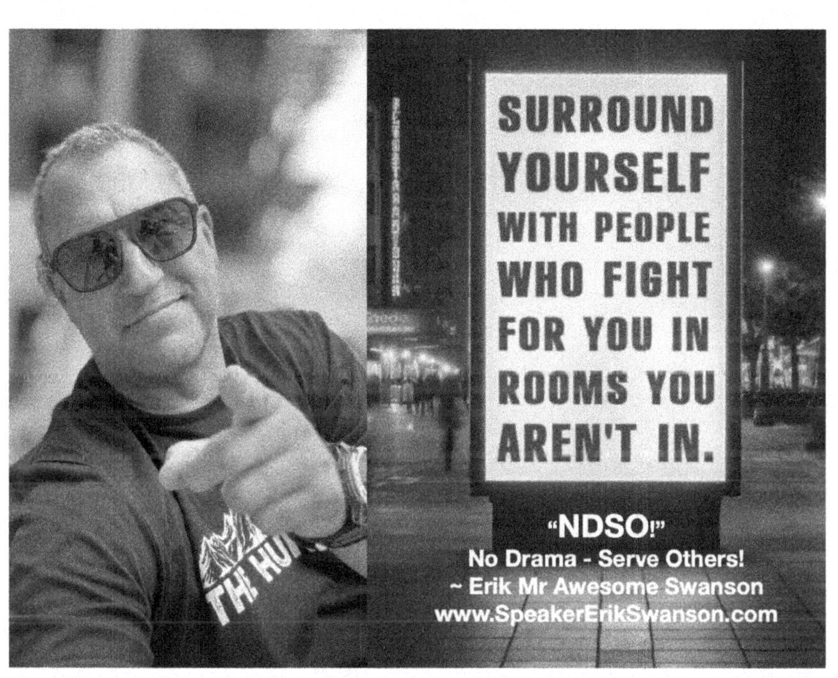
SURROUND
YOURSELF
WITH PEOPLE
WHO FIGHT
FOR YOU IN
ROOMS YOU
AREN'T IN.
"NDSO!"
No Drama - Serve Others!
~ Erik Mr Awesome Swanson
www.SpeakerErikSwanson.com